PRAISE FOR
THE STOWAWAY IN FIRST CLASS

"This book is more than a just a story of two young men coming to America as stowaways on an ocean liner from France in the early twentieth century. It is about how one individual, Guy, achieves the American dream that he set out to realize. Guy relies on . . . character, hard work, good personal relations, perseverance, and strong family ties to achieve his goal. It is also a story of human trafficking. It reads like a thriller. The author's riveting storytelling makes the book hard to put down."

—Ciro DeFalco, chairman, Casa Italiana Sociocultural Center, Inc./ Italian American Museum of Washington DC

"The harrowing story of Guy DeSantis as told by his son, is evidence that one decision can change your entire life. As Guy and his friend Ernesto stayed tucked away and out of sight in the bowels of the SS *Paris*, they had no idea how their journey would end. Their 'adventure' is worth the read, and the outcome will fill your heart with gratitude that out of one seemingly bad choice, good prevailed."

—Mindi Wroblewski, author of *The Paris Room* and *Your True Origin Story*

"A journey into a son's love for his father—a man who displayed incredible courage traveling into the unknown to a strange and frightening new promised land. A story about the strength of the family fabric in Italian culture. Thank you for the voyage."

—Soren Peter Dam, retired president, Colgate-Palmolive, Brazil

THE
Stowaway
in
First Class

SS *Paris*

THE
Stowaway
in
First Class

A True Story of an Unforgettable Quest to Come to America

Anthony DeSantis

FLAGSHIP PRESS

A Veritas Resurgence Book
Published by Flagship Press, Palm City, Florida
www.anthonydesantis.com

Designed by Girl Friday Productions
www.girlfridayproductions.com

Cover design: Emily Weigel
Project management: Kim Kent
Editorial production: Kylee Hayes
Photo Credits: Except where otherwise indicated, all photos are from the personal collection of Gaetano DeSantis, the author's personal collection, or from the public domain; p. 36 (top): SS *Paris* marketing brochure by Compagnie Generale Transatlantique; pp. 47 (top), 48 (top): historical collection at town hall, Arce, Italy; p. 67: map courtesy of Wikipedia; pp. 116 (bottom), 118: courtesy of Liliane Turlier; p. 129: courtesy of Rose Ferrari Treasures, Ancestry.com.

ISBN (hardcover): 979-8-9915110-0-1
ISBN (paperback): 979-8-9915110-1-8
ISBN (ebook): 979-8-9915110-2-5

Library of Congress Control Number: 2024921035

First edition

*To my father, an inspiration and example of humility,
who, in one generation, changed his legacy forever.*

Chi lascia la strada vecchia per la nuova, sa quel che lascia ma non sa quel che trova.

He who leaves the old way for the new, knows what he leaves but doesn't know what he will find.

—Old Italian Proverb

PROLOGUE

On March 5, 1929, at twenty-seven years old, my father faced a life-altering choice, the consequences of which would echo through generations. Had he known all the facts at the time, he would not have made the choice he did.

He began a journey that would change his family's entire future.

I heard the story countless times growing up and often shared the condensed version with my family and friends. Each time I told it, I got the same response:

"You have to write that story—it would make a great movie!"

The problem wasn't simply that I was not a writer, but that I had a family, two successful careers, and a busy life. While I always wanted to, I just never made the time. Like many of us with good intentions, life just got in the way. Then I arrived at a point in my life where time was no longer a valid excuse.

Fortunately, one year, while he was visiting, I did take the time to sit him in front of a video camera and record the story in his own words. I then accompanied him on a trip to Paris to visit the woman he'd left behind.

Then for thirty-seven years, I did nothing about it. I would retell his story over and over again, but I didn't write a word of it.

After a medical incident that almost ended my life, I realized the story of my father's incredible journey would have ended as well. The digital copy of the VCR tape I had made would be forgotten in the junk heap of files I would have left behind. Perhaps my wife, my children, and my sister had heard enough of the story to carry it on, but many of the details would be lost forever. It's time to write it down, at last.

The following story is true. The timeline and sequence of events as they occurred are real. My father could recall this story with amazing clarity. Although he was unable to fully verbalize what he experienced in vivid detail, his expressions told a much deeper story—one that I was fortunate enough to interpret over the years I spent listening to him. Each time, I imagined what he was thinking when he could not remember, by observing the passion in his voice or seeing the emotion in his face. I would ask him questions to bring out those feelings whenever I could. I succeeded in drawing out many of them. When I was not successful, I would paint the scene in my mind based on those facial expressions or the inflection in his voice as he described it to me. I attempted to fill the gaps whenever I could.

In writing his story, I have tried to capture those emotions—those expressions—and tell it in the way he would want it to be told.

While some names of the people involved have been changed to protect their privacy, the events are as true as I can remember them or as he described them to me. Any inaccuracies or discrepancies in the dates and places are solely my responsibility.

The book before you is the result of God's gift to me of a restored life. He graciously granted me another chance, the time to research the full story, and most importantly, the vision to write it. Whether or not it makes for a good movie is for others to decide.

My intent is to present a heartfelt and accurate account of the events that took place in my father's life one hundred years ago—not only so my grandchildren can learn and appreciate the important lessons passed on to them from their courageous great-grandfather—but so the children and grandchildren of immigrants everywhere will find strength and encouragement from his story of coming to America with nothing and creating a wonderful life for himself and his family.

Anthony DeSantis
Palm City, Florida
July 2023

CHAPTER 1

The turbulence rocked my sleep, though it was completely imaginary. The flight had been exceptionally smooth, but how could I sleep dwelling on how this weekend would play out for my father? How would he explain to Marie why he'd just disappeared so long ago? Even though he wrote to her many times after he arrived in America, she never replied to his letters. He assumed she had moved on. The uncertainty had always bothered him.

The rattle of the breakfast service on this all-night flight shook me from my jet-lagged, stormy slumber. It was clear the flight attendant serving our first-class section had been around awhile and was one of the best. She appeared to be in her late fifties, well-groomed, with a warm, professional demeanor. She knew we were traveling standby, yet she treated us like full-paying first-class passengers, without a hint of indifference or condescension.

Dad had awakened and stared out his window seat into the dawn-colored sky. I doubted he looked at anything, but I could see his mind was on meeting Marie as well. Would she be waiting for him as she promised? If so, what would Dad say? What could he say? After all, it had been fifty-seven years since he had left her without saying good-bye, and he had not seen or spoken to her since. Recently they had exchanged letters after he received her address from a mutual friend, who had seen Marie while on vacation in France. All they knew of each other was they had lost their spouses many years before. My father wanted to see her again. Why had she now graciously agreed to see him?

The flight attendant offered us coffee and the usual selection of first-class entrees for breakfast. Dad chose the cheese omelet—but knowing better, I stuck with my usual choice of cereal and fruit. There was not much that the food-service department could do to ruin a banana and a box of Cheerios.

"Are you nervous, Dad?" I asked.

He turned to me with his gentle smile and shook his head. I was not expecting much more explanation.

"I'm not nervous about seeing her. I just hope she'll understand why I left."

"But you explained that to her in a letter after you arrived in America," I said.

"I did. But I never heard back from her. Maybe she never got it."

I heard the hesitation in his voice—he was nervous. In all the years I've witnessed, nothing bothered him. He was a quiet, soft-spoken man of few words, very typical of the Italian men I had known and read about from the *Mezzogiorno*, The Land of the Midday Sun—the southern part of Italy—who had immigrated to the US in the early twentieth century. He had what the Italians called *pazienza*—patience—for sure, a quiet self-assurance, and control of his emotions. I witnessed that continually in my childhood, especially since my mother was at the opposite end of the spectrum when it came to emotional expression.

Like my father, she was kind and loving, but when we did something that upset her, she did not hesitate to let us know in a fiery, hand-waving tirade. This would often be accompanied by Italian words and phrases, which I learned were quite colorful and common in Italy, but not suitable for everyday use in America, especially not in elementary school. Much of my early Italian vocabulary came from listening to my mom rant and rave. My friends and I laughed along with her at her many sarcastic expressions in English as well.

"Run up a tree and branch off" was one of her favorites.

"Take the gas pipe," she would say when she was upset with me. I never figured out what that really meant, although from her tone I got the idea.

My father, however, did not typify the stereotypical image of the brash, tough Italian men we all saw on TV or in the movies. His only concern was the well-being of his family, not what others thought of him, or how masculine he appeared to his Italian friends. The quiet, determined calmness with which he lived his life reflected that strength of character. Now, at eighty-four, he exhibited those qualities even more.

We both enjoyed our breakfast choices, and Dad cleaned his plate. As a typical Italian, eating was an important part of the day. Mother was an excellent cook. We always ate well at our house. To Dad, even an airline meal was something to be savored and enjoyed when you were hungry. We had not eaten since dinner, served right after takeoff ten hours earlier.

The jumbo jet rumbled almost imperceptibly, and the pilot reduced power to begin a gentle descent. Most of the passengers did not even notice the slight change in noise level. I'm a pilot, trained to listen for even the slightest variations in engine noise. I noticed it. It signaled that we were about thirty minutes from landing, close to the moment I had anxiously feared.

Dad never had the opportunity to fly with me when I was part of the flight crew, but it thrilled me to be able to accompany him on this trip. It was a chance for me to experience a part of the extraordinary story he had been telling me all these years. For him, he was adding another chapter, but it would be a chapter unlike the one which started it all.

The seat belt sign illuminated with its accompanying chime.

"Ladies and gentlemen, this is the captain speaking. We have started our descent for landing at Paris Orly Airport and will be landing soon. The weather in Paris is clear with a temperature of 11 degrees Celsius, 52 degrees Fahrenheit. Thank you for flying with us today, and we hope you enjoyed your flight."

To think that one day I could be making that exact announcement was hard for me to imagine. I was thirty-eight at the time and had been with the airline for only ten years. Sure, the captains that I had flown with had allowed me to make some PA announcements as a copilot on our domestic route system, but I was not yet senior enough to fly on international flights. Announcing our arrival into Buffalo was just not the same. It wasn't lost on me that I would probably not be flying at all if it were not for this man sitting next to me and another flight across the Atlantic that had landed in Paris many years before.

Fifty-nine years earlier, my father stood with about one hundred and fifty thousand other excited spectators at Le Bourget Aerodrome, seven miles northeast of Paris, anxiously awaiting the arrival of "Lucky Lindy" in the Spirit of St. Louis. Charles Lindbergh had left Long Island in New York the previous day and landed at 10:22 p.m. on May 27, 1927, after thirty-three and a half hours of flying. According to press reports, the roads leading to Le Bourget that day were crammed with cars, taxis, and buses. It was as though everyone in Paris showed up to watch this historic event. People stood in taxis that had sliding roof-top panels, or on the open buses and trolleys, drank wine and champagne, and passed bottles to each other in celebration. Floodlights on the ground illuminated the field, and other planes circled the skies over Le Bourget to welcome him. One by one, those planes landed, and after he circled the Eiffel Tower, Lindbergh touched down, the first pilot to successfully complete a solo nonstop flight across the Atlantic.

For the next few days, free food and liquor were given out at establishments all over town and people partied in the street. Dad vividly described the chaos of that day and told me about the small pictures of Lindbergh that everyone purchased. How could he know that one day I would fly for an airline that would claim Charles Lindbergh as one of its original pilots, and flights across the Atlantic would be commonplace?

The feelings that overcame my father as he witnessed that historic event fired in him an enthusiastic interest in flight that he unknowingly passed on to me. He told me the story numerous times, each time as enthusiastically as the time before. His favorite weekend trip, and eventually mine as well, was driving to the local airfield a few miles from our house to watch small airplanes take off and land on a grass runway. On many Sundays, instead of going to Fenway Park to watch baseball, to the beach, or to visit his *paesanos*—his friends in the Italian suburbs of Boston—we would spend the afternoon on the outdoor decks overlooking the terminals at Boston's Logan Airport. There were no glass partitions, no security gates, or other restrictions. We were able to just stand there, peer over the wall, and gaze at the beautiful planes, the pilots in their impressive uniforms, and the well-dressed passengers just a few feet in front of us on the tarmac. As a young boy, I was enamored with the whole experience. Little did I or my father know that my future as a commercial pilot was already in its formative stage.

"Is there anything else you want to tell me, Dad, before I put this cassette tape recorder away?"

"No," he said, "it's the same story that I told you before. Nothing new."

I had spent an hour with him after takeoff, reviewing what I knew already and preparing him so he could recall it all accurately for Marie.

"What about Marie? What does she look like?" I asked.

"I don't remember much," he replied with a look of apology. "It's been a long time."

He did recall that she was shorter than he was, which would have put her less than Dad's modest five-foot six-inch frame. He described her short black hair and her pretty face, which I remembered seeing from a group photo of her at Marie's cousin Philomena's wedding that took place in November 1928. In the picture, they were standing together, but since she was only sixteen, and he was twenty-seven, it probably was not her father's favorite picture. He did not approve of the relationship. Dad was too old for his daughter.

What always struck me in the picture were two things. First, no one was smiling except for maybe one lady in the back row next to the accordion player, but even that wasn't much of a smile. The rest of the wedding party and guests had serious looks on their faces, including the bride and groom. It looked more like a funeral than a wedding to me.

The other was Dad sporting a large pompadour hairstyle. It was combed into a mound in front, about three or four inches high, and very wavy. When I first saw the picture, I thought it looked funny—although, no one else was laughing. That hairstyle was obviously a current trend for men, and he seemed proud of how it made him look in his fancy suit and bow tie. I remember thinking he must have been a real ladies' man back then, but I've never witnessed that part of him. Even now, he still had lots of hair, gray, and thinning in spots—at his age it made him look handsome.

Dad told me Marie should be waiting for us in the international arrival hall at the bottom of the ramp we would use.

"But how will we know what she looks like after all these years?" I asked.

Fortunately, he had asked her that in the letter, anticipating their shared apprehension.

"She said she will be standing with a newspaper tucked under one arm and holding a rose with the other," Dad said. She would now be about seventy-three years old.

I kept hoping she would be there. Maybe this would answer whatever questions were still in her mind as well. Why did he leave? Why hadn't he ever come back?

Surely, she already knew the answers, didn't she? He couldn't be sure. Had she even read the letters? Did she even care? He was about to get those answers.

My silent prayer was that he would not be hurt by what he would soon find out.

*The Wedding Picture (1928). Marie is above the right shoulder
of the bride. Gaetano is standing on her right.*

CHAPTER 2

As we continued our initial descent, Dad noticed that one of the pilots had been sitting back with us in first class. And he wanted to know why. As a copilot flying the same airplane, the DC-10, I knew there were four pilots assigned to the flight crew on long flights such as this, so I wasn't alarmed to see one of them in his designated crew rest seat. My simple explanation calmed him, and the look in his eyes reflected his pride in me.

"Flight attendants prepare for landing" rang out over the PA, and my thoughts returned to what was about to happen to my father. Now, even I was nervous.

Dad had slept for most of the flight, but when he was awake, he seemed lost in thought, often staring out the window. Other than the daily newspaper, he was not much of a reader. He had taught himself to read and write in English from his native Italian tongue. He could also speak French, which he had learned during the five years he lived there. Reading was a struggle for him, and he didn't need a book to entertain himself. He was simply fascinated with the thrill of flying.

I watched him for a few seconds and thought about how much I admired this man with a fourth-grade education, who had always encouraged me to work hard, do well in school, and get a college education.

"You can do much better than me," was a phrase I would often remember him saying very clearly when I found myself struggling to do just that—do much better than he did. Whenever I thought life was getting difficult and thoughts of quitting college played tricks on me, I would think of him, and how proud he had been when I received the appointment to the US Air Force Academy.

In just one generation, he had experienced life in America as a poor Italian immigrant—who had entered the country illegally—to now having a son with an opportunity to graduate from a prestigious military academy in his new country. Mom and Dad had saved a few thousand dollars toward my college education, but I would need so much more in loans and scholarships to attend any of the schools I had applied to. When his adopted country offered to provide me an education worth over $250,000 at the school of my dreams, he knew he had accomplished what he had set out to do when he left Italy—start a new and better life for himself and his future family. The struggles he had gone through to get here would have all been worth it.

There was no way I was going to let him down.

He adjusted his gray tweed sport jacket and tugged on his blue striped tie—which he wore not only because a tie was required for all non-revs in first class—but because it was how he dressed to travel most places away from home, especially to a city like Paris. His normal daily attire before he retired had consisted of old work clothes—a pair of worn-out cotton pants, a flannel shirt that had seen better days, hard-toe construction boots, and a metal lunch box, just what you would expect for a man who spent his life in America as a construction laborer working outside all day. During the week—in rain, snow, hot weather or cold—he would build beautiful brick walls or help prepare the ground to pave roads or parking lots. On some weekends, he even did gardening and landscaping for his boss at the sand and gravel company. Carrying my own metal lunch box, I often got to join him on Saturdays and witnessed how hard he worked. He would describe his job simply as "pick and shovel."

It was the only work most of the Italian immigrants of that era could find. In our neighborhood in the Italian section of town, all of my friends' fathers who had immigrated worked in either carpentry or construction. It was excruciatingly hard, and the wages were incredibly low. My father would come home at the end of the week, physically exhausted, handing my mother his measly paycheck. At the time, however, my sister and I thought that it was a lot of money. He never let on that it was barely enough for us to scrape by for another week, and my frugal mom always made it last. Along with the tips she received as a waitress at a local Italian restaurant, she even had some left over to put into savings. I still remember accompanying her to the bank each week so she could deposit one dollar into our Christmas Club accounts. No interest was paid, of course, but in fifty weeks, they had saved enough for our gifts.

Before the descent, Dad had shaved and freshened up and was ready to meet Marie. I had carefully stowed the cassette recorder and tapes under my seat. Most of the answers he gave to my questions were not new or revealing, but it was reassuring to know I had recorded the story accurately as he told it to me again. As a boy, I had heard him tell it so many times to friends and family at night from my tiny bedroom off of the kitchen of our small apartment. My bedroom was smaller than a normal size bathroom, and it didn't even have a regular door—only a flimsy folding closet door made of vinyl—and I heard everything.

Hopefully, during the next few days there would be many more questions answered and new details to add to his remarkable journey. Having also freshened up a bit prior to the descent, I put on my shoes. I was ready.

The landing was smooth and uneventful, just as I tried to make them when I sat at the controls. We slowly taxied to the arrival gate, and most of the passengers busily gathered their belongings, stowed their reading material, and put on their shoes. Dad didn't have to do any of that.

We followed the line of passengers out of the plane. Since we had been in the front cabin, the line to the customs and immigration counters was short. We retrieved our luggage and were checked through customs without having to endure a physical inspection. The few bags we had with us were light. Our plan was to spend the weekend in Paris with Marie and her family, then continue to Italy by train, where I would spend a week with my Italian relatives and fly home to California from there. Dad would stay in Italy for another month to have lots of time to catch up on family news and reacquaint with his two half-sisters and two half-brothers. He hadn't seen any of them in ten years.

As we headed into the arrivals terminal, we could see hundreds of people jockeying for position around the exit ramp, anxiously looking for their loved ones to appear. I was glad Dad and Marie had thought of this ahead of time, but even so, it would be difficult to find any particular person in such a large, noisy crowd. Calling out a name wasn't going to work. We weren't even certain she would be there.

Dad noticed an older, well-dressed woman standing next to what appeared to be a niece or daughter, both anxiously looking up the ramp. She had short, black hair, but he could not remember her face. Since it had certainly changed over the years, it could have been her.

Then he noticed the rose.

In her right hand she had a single, red rose and under her left arm was the folded newspaper. It had to be Marie. He pointed her out to me. He waved. Marie waved back. When they made eye contact and realized they were seeing each other for the first time in fifty-seven years, my father's eyes watered and a big smile appeared on his face. Marie beamed, like she was greeting an old friend returning from a long summer vacation.

As we walked down the ramp, the relief and emotion affected me as well, and I felt tears forming in my eyes. I was so happy for my father that—so far—this trip was working out well.

As we continued to walk toward her, my thoughts drifted back to the day when the stranger approached my father in Paris, the day he left, the day his life would change forever—and it would change my destiny as well.

That fateful day had started the chain of events that had led him back to her today.

CHAPTER 3

Fortunately for Gaetano, or Guy as he liked to be called, the weather in Paris in March of 1929 had turned from the cold dreariness of winter to the crisp, cool days of spring. The shift would certainly become a factor for him later that day, although he didn't know it yet. As he did every day, he walked home from the jobsite to have lunch. Only on this beautiful, sunny day, when he arrived home, his landlord, Alberto, had some unexpected news for him.

"Hey, Gaetano, there was someone here looking for you," he said.

"Did you know who it was?" Guy asked.

"No, I've never seen him before. I told him you would be back at 5:30, and the man said he would return then because he needed to see you today."

Alberto was not only his landlord but also his boss on the construction site and a good friend. It was Alberto who had written to Guy when he was living in Southern France and had originally offered Guy the job in Paris and a place to stay. They had known each other from their younger days in Italy. Alberto was from the town of Casalvieri, not far from where Guy grew up in Arce.

The room he rented with another friend was small but comfortable. Alberto's wife, Angela, was an exceptionally good cook and served them great lunches and dinners as part of his room and board each day. Guy also enjoyed their companionship and being around their two little girls and a boy. He felt part of a family. He was happy there.

Guy tried to enjoy his lunch but was troubled by the thought that someone had come to the house and specifically asked to see him. And he needed to see him today. Hopefully, he was not in some kind of trouble. He couldn't think of any. Maybe something had happened to his family back home. All kinds of possible scenarios went through his head. None of them were good. If there was a death or medical emergency involving one of his parents, why hadn't he received a telegram from Italy? Whatever it was, he told himself, it would have to wait until he got home later.

After a quick lunch, he walked back to his job and worked a normal shift that day, operating a crane. Guy enjoyed the work of simply manipulating several control levers in front of him much more than the heavy manual labor jobs he had held in the past. But he also knew that one careless mistake could get someone hurt. He focused on the potentially dangerous work at hand, but he couldn't shake the thought of this stranger looking for him. Was his family all right? What could this be about?

When the workday was over, Guy hurried home so he would not miss seeing this man again. He arrived home and had just enough time to get cleaned up and to change into some fresh clothes when the stranger showed up.

Alberto was already home, and he pointed out the window of their front door and said, "That's the man who came earlier."

Guy had never seen this man before either, so he cautiously went outside to meet him.

"Are you Gaetano DeSantis?" the man asked.

"Yes, that's me. Who are you?"

"Do you have a cousin in the United States by the name of Frank DeSantis?" He never identified himself.

"Yes, I do," answered Guy, relieved that at least it didn't involve his family in Italy. What would Frank have to do with it? He hadn't heard from Frank in months when they had last exchanged letters.

"Does he work in a bakery?"

"Yes."

"And he lives in the town of Newton, Massachusetts?"

"Yes, that's right. What's this all about?" Guy was frustrated with all the questions and no answers.

"Did you know that your cousin wants you to come to the United States?"

That question took him by surprise. Guy had been writing to Frank about the possibility of joining him in America, but they hadn't specifically discussed it in several years. He had often thought about going to America, to join Frank and his other friends who had left Italy during the mass immigration period of the early 1920s. They had endured the arduous journey in steerage class to achieve a better life.

It had been a dream of Guy's ever since he first heard from his cousin about how much better life was for him in the United States. Frank often enticed Guy with stories about his neighborhood, his many Italian American friends, his job in the bakery, and his pay. Guy imagined being able to send money regularly to help his family in Italy. He knew he would not have that kind of opportunity by staying on the farm, or by staying in Italy. It's what motivated Guy to move to France when he had the chance.

But that had been five years ago. As Frank was writing to Guy, describing the steps to take to come to America, everything changed. The United States restricted immigration by enacting the Immigration Act of 1924, and it appeared that there was little to discuss. Unlike when Frank made the journey, Guy would now have to obtain a visa from a US consulate before being allowed to enter the country. All Frank had to do was prove he could work and not be a burden to the US.

As long as you were listed on the ship's manifest and could pass a relatively simple battery of medical and physical tests at Ellis Island, you were allowed into the country. Guy knew the law had basically closed the door to "undesirables," including immigrants from Southern and Eastern Europe, especially Southern Italians with no skills to offer. He knew he was considered one of those "undesirables," as many Italians were cast as unwanted in America and treated with disrespect and low-class status. There was no way he could get a visa.

"Yes, we talked about it, but not in a while."

The man then introduced himself as Michel and showed Guy that he had an American passport. Guy could tell by his accent that he was also Italian, but since he lived in France, he went by the French name Mee-SHELL instead of his given Italian name, Mi-KEL-eh.

"Your cousin has already paid for everything for you to go to the United States. You won't have to pay anything at all. You'll just have to come with me tonight and get onto the boat. It will leave for New York tomorrow. Your cousin will be waiting for you there."

Guy could not believe what he had just heard. How could his cousin arrange this without letting him know? The whole idea seemed incredible to him. Why hadn't Frank written to him about this? Having seen Michel's American passport, he was willing to believe that Michel knew his cousin Frank. But why the sudden urgency?

"Can't we go another time?" he said.

"No, you have to come with me tonight."

Guy thought for a moment. Was this real or a setup? His mind was a blur.

There was no way he could just leave. He would have to go to Italy first and tell his parents. Some of his belongings were still there and he would have to get those. Plus, he liked it here in Paris. There was no reason for him to leave now. He had found a nice life here, good friends, and a decent job that was depending on him. Even though it was a dream he continued to embrace, he had given up any hope of ever achieving it. He hadn't thought about going to America in an exceptionally long time.

"But I can't go tonight," Guy retorted emphatically.

Even if he wanted to go to America, there were other issues he had to consider.

"I have money in the bank here, which I'll have to withdraw. I need to get paid for the work I've already done on this job. I can't *just* leave!"

Guy knew right away that Michel was offering to take him to America as a stowaway. Without a passport or a visa, it was the only way he could get on a boat to America. It would be a frightful way to get there.

The trip was shorter now, as the boats were faster and steerage class had been mostly eliminated, but to have to hide out in a boat for even a week was unimaginable. He had heard stories of other men who had tried being stowaways on their own. Most of them were unsuccessful, and they were either sent back or put in jail.

There was just no other way it could be done. Frank had obviously paid someone to bring him over illegally. The idea frightened him. What if it didn't work? What if he was caught? Was he willing to risk his life or his future on such little information?

"No," Michel replied sternly. "Your cousin paid for this trip. If you don't come with me tonight, he'll lose all the money he has already paid for you to go."

The thought of Frank losing all that money suddenly overrode Guy's objections because he knew his cousin must have paid quite a lot for this. Criminals such as Michel and the people he was likely associated with would not take those kinds of chances unless there was some serious profit in it.

Could it be related to the Black Hand Society in America—*la Mano Nera*? He had heard stories about the extortion rings and kidnapping schemes that those organized groups in America were involved in. Especially during the early 1900s, the Black Hand had terrorized Italian neighborhoods in New York, Chicago, and other American cities by the tens of thousands. They demanded money from business owners who—if they did not comply—were threatened with watching their buildings and businesses burn. They kidnapped children and held them for weeks until their parents could produce substantial ransom payments.

Members of the gangs were secretly hired as bank tellers, acting as moles, and getting access to the names and transactions of merchants who had done well financially so that these people could be terrorized. Its members also gathered around bars, restaurants, social clubs, and barbershops, collecting gossip on acquaintances who had recently married, who had recently died and left money to their children, who had family back in the old country wanting to come to America, or who had recently sold their house or property back in Italy.

Certainly, Frank would have no part in any of that. Guy refused to believe that his cousin engaged in any illegal activities. But maybe someone was extorting Frank and had demanded money from him to secure Guy's passage or had even threatened Frank's life, or Guy's safety. He couldn't be sure of any of that and had no time or means of verifying any of it.

He assumed that it must have cost his cousin at least a half year's salary as a baker, based on what it would actually cost to travel to the United States legally by ship in those days. How had he earned that kind of money? Guy could not bear the thought of his cousin losing that much if he refused the offer. He was frightened, confused, and upset. What should he do? A decision had to be made now. It had to be tonight or nothing!

"It's up to you whether you want him to lose all that money," the man said, affirming the same thoughts Guy was debating in his mind.

That did it. Guy could not believe what he was about to say. These three words changed his life forever.

"Okay, I'll come."

It was irrational. There were so many questions, but he just didn't have time to get the answers. His decision was based strictly on the obligation he felt to his cousin. He would just have to believe this stranger and hope that what he was saying was true. Frank would be there waiting for him. How could he disappoint his cousin with such a refusal?

Francesco DeSantis—Frank—had gone to America in 1921, eight years before, when he was just seventeen years old. Guy was living in Italy at the time, and he clearly remembered when Frank left. Guy was two years older than Frank, but they were close, still sharing the bond they had from childhood. Their fathers were brothers, and they spent many days running around their grandfather's farm together. They had written to each other many times since Frank left, and Guy believed that his cousin would do whatever he could to get him to America.

But this?

He had not heard from Frank for a few months, and he had never told Frank that he was ready to leave France to come to the United States. This stranger had assured him that Frank would be waiting for him in New York. Why else would these people risk taking him on a ship as a stowaway if Frank hadn't already paid them?

"I have to go tell my boss and quit my job."

Guy still didn't know much about Michel other than he had an American passport but thought it best not to press that issue. Maybe he didn't want to know. Michel said he was staying at a hotel nearby but would come back shortly to pick Guy up.

"Don't take anything. Don't pack a suitcase. Nothing. Just the suit you have and some stuff for shaving. That's it."

Guy stepped back into the house and sat dejectedly with his boss. He told Alberto what the stranger wanted and that he had made the decision to go to the United States because his cousin had already paid for it. He had to leave tonight. The news shocked his boss. He understood what Guy was telling him—that he was about to undertake an illegal and very risky voyage as a stowaway. Alberto would be losing not only a good worker, and the income from a good tenant, but he was losing a good friend as well. He promised to send Guy his accrued pay once he had an address in America. He would have Guy's pay sent to a bank in the United States with the required paperwork signed by an attorney.

Somewhat relieved, but still in shock at the turn of events he had experienced in the last few hours, Guy went to his room to start packing the few things he would be allowed to take with him. The boarder who shared the room with Guy wanted to know what was going on.

Ernesto Zaino, from Sora, a small town in Italy not far from Guy's hometown, worked for a different company in Paris, but they had become friends.

"I'm leaving tonight," Guy said.

Ernesto was incredulous.

"What? Where are you going?"

"To the United States. A guy came to see me today and told me that my cousin in America had already paid for the trip. He's coming to get me tonight to take me to a boat, which will be leaving tomorrow."

Ernesto was intrigued by what Guy was telling him. Even the fact that he would be going as a stowaway didn't seem to bother Ernesto, which surprised Guy. Why the interest? He, too, worked in construction as a cement finisher but hadn't been as happy in Paris as Guy was. Ernesto had often talked about going to America.

What Guy didn't know was that Ernesto had been a stowaway before. He had been caught and sent back to Italy, but the lure of the American dream had not left him. He wouldn't try doing it again on his own, but what if someone now were to help him?

He asked a few more questions, briefly thought about it, and found out from Guy where Michel was staying. Ernesto ran off to pay him a visit.

"Is there any chance I could go too? I want to go to America," he told Michel.

"Who do you have that lives in the United States?"

"I have a brother."

"Where does your brother live?"

"He lives in Detroit."

Michel was surprised at this unexpected request and very skeptical.

"Do you have a letter or some other proof that your brother is living there?"

"Yes, I have some letters he wrote to me. I'll find them for you."

He dug through the papers he had brought with him and showed him a letter from his brother with his address in Detroit. Michel studied the letter and return address very carefully.

After a few moments, he looked up at Ernesto.

"Well, if you want to, you can come too."

Ernesto rushed back to tell Guy. They looked at each other and burst out laughing at the craziness of the idea. Guy felt a tinge of excitement. What were they about to do? Although he was thankful to know that he would now have some companionship on this venture, it didn't reassure him that it was the right choice.

Why had Michel agreed to take Ernesto as well? Maybe Frank had paid them enough to cover the costs for Ernesto too. Or maybe he was just assuming that Ernesto's brother would pay willingly once he arrived in New York. The more they discussed it, the harder they laughed, relieving the tension Guy was feeling.

Alberto was about to lose both of his boarders. He had been a good friend to both men and wanted to help.

"Well, Gaetano," he said, "if you don't make it and you have to come back, the job is all yours."

Guy thanked him for all he had done, and they said good-bye—hugging and kissing on both cheeks, as was the Italian custom. He thanked Angela for all the good cooking he had enjoyed. He embraced the children.

What about all the other friends he would be leaving behind? He wouldn't be able to say good-bye to them. The sadness of it all overwhelmed whatever sense of excitement he allowed himself to entertain.

He assumed Alberto would tell some of his close friends he had left

Paris, but he wouldn't want the details to get around the community. Guy had never intentionally broken the law in his life, and he especially didn't want his friends to know that he was about to do something illegal. He told himself he would write to them and his family in Italy as soon as he was able to, assuming that he made it safely to America.

Then he realized he did not have time to see Marie to tell her he was leaving.

It was already time to go.

Next page: The "family" boarding house in Paris (circa 1928). Ernesto (left), Alberto (center), and Gaetano (right). Angela and the children.

CHAPTER 4

As promised, Michel returned a few hours later in a black sedan. The driver paid no attention to the new passengers as they got into the vehicle and drove off to the train station. Guy and Ernesto had each stuffed a small brown paper bag with a razor and some soap into a suit pocket just as they were told. Their sudden and unplanned journey, what little they knew of it, began with a short drive during normal traffic, but it would soon spin into something very unusual.

Both said nothing, but the tension in the air was noticeable. None of the details of how they would get to America were discussed, except for one. They would attempt to stowaway aboard the French ocean liner, SS *Paris*, docked in Le Havre, about 150 miles away.

The driver dropped them off at the station at Gare Saint-Lazare, the first train station built in Paris. It was a beautiful, artistic building that opened in 1837, ninety-two years prior. Train travel was common, but most Parisians had not used it for anything but local services to the western suburbs of the city. This grand old station also served cities as far away as Normandy using the Paris-Le Havre railway, on which they would travel. The three men sat together, engaging in light and congenial conversation but did not discuss any of the details of what they were about to do when they arrived in Le Havre.

As the train clattered along on the old tracks, the men gazed out the windows. It was already getting dark, and there was little to see of the new countryside. The route, however, was very scenic through the picturesque French vineyards and villages, crossing the river Seine several times at Asnières and again at Houilles. Near Rouen, it crossed it again at Oissel. After crossing central Rouen, the train passed through the town of Yvetot, and finally, about three hours after leaving Paris, it arrived at the main station in Le Havre.

The Port of Le Havre, created as a French state agency in 1920, was just a short distance from the train station. Founded as a port in 1517, it was one of the largest in France, both in terms of passenger ships and freight. Although parts of the city looked old and in need of renovation, there were many new structures built to accommodate the increasing number of ships using the port for its strategic location on the English Channel. The area around the harbor itself bustled with traffic, and there were many hotels and restaurants catering to the thousands of people using it for travel to various parts of the world each day.

Guy and Ernesto bought a few things to eat at the station and packed a small sack with cheese, bread, and a bottle of wine to take with them. Michel had said that might be all they would get to eat until the following morning. Then they boarded a cab for the short two-mile drive to the pier. Guy noticed that there was a boat parked at the dock, but it was not the SS *Paris*. Then he saw a ship anchored offshore. That had to be the *Paris*. Since it was not leaving until morning, he assumed it would be brought to the dock once the other ship had left, and boarding would take place from there. He had no idea what was about to happen.

Michel instructed Guy and Ernesto to follow him but to get no closer than twenty-five feet from him or from each other. As they carefully followed him to a beach-like shoreline, they could see the ship parked in the water in the distance. Guy had never before seen anything that big and wondered how they were going to get onto the ship from the water. Maybe there was a ladder or stairs to climb. Perhaps there was an entry hatch they could access near the water line. Then they noticed a small rowboat with two men apparently waiting for them. Michel led them to this rowboat and said he would leave them now.

"Buon voyage," he said. "We'll see you."

The two young men thought it was strange that Michel was leaving them already but said nothing of it and bid good-bye to their escort.

After nervously getting on the rowboat, they made their way toward the ship. The night air was pleasantly cool, but the ocean was rough, and the waves lapped the little rowboat as they slowly and quietly got closer and closer.

It was almost eleven by now, very dark, and there were no lights in the cabins. Since there were no passengers onboard, it was also quiet on the decks. It appeared that the crew was asleep, resting in preparation for the long workdays that would keep them busy for the next few weeks. Maybe some of them had gone off the ship to enjoy some free time and nightlife in Le Havre. Only a single bright light illuminated the top of the ship, but they could clearly see the outline of the entire ship.

As they reached the ship, one of the two men—both French—grabbed the anchor chain and pulled them closer to it. He then stepped onto it and began to climb it. That's when the terrifying realization struck Guy that this was the way the Frenchmen had planned to get them on the ship. They would have to climb the anchor line!

The Frenchman on the anchor chain said, "I'll go first, and you both follow me up." The other man would stay behind in the rowboat.

Guy worried that he would not be able to do it. He couldn't believe that's how they had planned to get them onboard. The chain was made of some sort of heavy-duty steel, so he wasn't concerned it would break. Each link of the chain was about two feet in length, consisting of two one-foot sections separated by another steel crossbar. However, the width of the chain appeared only wide enough to get a shoe into the link. If he miscalculated at all, he would not have a secure step to pull himself up.

Guy couldn't swim. He was terrified. Ernesto stepped onto the chain after the Frenchman, and Guy swallowed his fear and put his foot into the link. His shoe just fit. The chain looked like it was about fifty feet in length, a long climb for sure. That meant he would have to step into each link and onto each crossbar about fifty times. How was he ever going to make it?

His only thought was, *Don't look down.*

Slowly, they climbed the chain—still wearing their suits—one link at a time. Guy was carrying the food sack, which made the climb more difficult, and he took as much time as he needed to be certain of his footing. He kept looking up, and he finally saw Ernesto step into the anchor bay and off the chain. He knew he could make it now. Just a few more links to go. He finally stepped into the anchor bay himself and felt relieved. He had made it. They had been quiet and it seemed no one had seen them climbing the chain. The anchor bay, used to secure the anchor to the side of the ship once it was raised, had a space large enough for Guy to crawl through to the inside of the ship. Once inside, the men found themselves in a room that stored the chain and housed the machinery used to deploy and retrieve the heavy anchor. A stairway from that room led up to the top deck of the ship. There was no activity on the top deck.

The Frenchman led them to a secluded corner of the deck. He pointed to the chain and told them he would go back down but said, "You stay here, and somebody will come later tonight or tomorrow morning to get you and bring you to where you need to go."

That did not sit well with Guy after what he had just been through.

"Wait. What if he doesn't come? Then what are we to do?"

The Frenchman looked at them with a questioning expression but had no answer.

Guy realized they would now be on the ship by themselves, hiding in the dark. They wouldn't know anyone. At least while they were on the rowboat, they had someone with them, someone to rely on if things didn't go well. Just when he thought the hard part was over, the threat of being alone and vulnerable on this big ship generated a renewed sense of fright for Guy, and he cursed the men who had put them in this position. He cursed himself for being so naive and foolish.

"We have no idea if anyone will come."

Ernesto added, "I don't like this."

They both agreed that the situation was unacceptable. If they were left alone and someone found them, they could be thrown off the boat or worse, put in jail. Both men told the Frenchman that they didn't want to stay on the ship alone.

Reluctantly, the Frenchman said, "Well, if you want to go back, we'll go back." Fortunately for them, the French guy was a pleasant fellow, didn't argue with them, and understood their predicament. He told them he didn't want them to worry about staying alone on the ship and agreed to escort them back to shore.

But first, they had to get back down the anchor chain.

Guy had made it up the chain by continually looking at Ernesto ahead and above him. He tried to constantly keep his eyes on the ship, not the water below. Now on his way back down, he had to look to make sure he secured his footing in the links below. As he did so, the water was all he saw. He knew that if he fell, he would be like a stone and would go right to the bottom. There was no one there to break his fall or to catch him. He wasn't physically shaking, but he was terrified. How had they ever agreed to this?

Each step down the chain was very methodical and took a long time. Guy was afraid to lift his foot off the chain he was on until he was positive that his foot was secure in the next link. After what seemed to take forever, they made it to the bottom and stepped into the rowboat that had been waiting for the other Frenchman to return. The night air was getting cooler, but it had not been a problem thus far. They rowed quietly to the shore. Michel was still there waiting.

"What happened?" he asked disappointedly.

Guy was angry. "Look," he said. "We're not criminals trying to escape. We didn't kill anybody. So we're not going to stay on that boat not knowing whether anybody was ever going to come for us. We both have good jobs in Paris. We've decided that we're not going to go to the United States. We want to go back to Paris."

"Why have you changed your mind?" Michel asked incredulously. "What didn't you like?" He still hadn't understood the terror of the whole ordeal for these men.

Guy explained to him that if someone had stayed on the boat to make sure the right people had come for them, it might have been different. They probably would have stayed and waited. But to leave them alone—without anyone there to protect or vouch for them on the ship—was not acceptable.

"But there was nobody. We were left by ourselves. Tomorrow we'll take the train back to Paris," Guy said.

Michel tried to calm them down and change their minds, but he could tell the two men were frightened. Trying to convince them to climb the anchor chain again was not going to work.

"Okay," he finally said. "Let's see if we can find a place to spend the night at a hotel tonight. Tomorrow, we'll meet at eight o'clock and go back to the boat. This time we'll go in like the other people but dressed as workers as part of the crew."

"No, no," they both said. "We've already made our decision."

Michel ignored the assertion and changed the subject.

"Would you be comfortable staying at a hotel by yourself?" he asked.

"No," they both said. At this hour of the night, in a strange city, and a shady part of town, it, too, sounded like another bad idea.

Grudgingly, Michel said he would go along too. However, it was impossible to find a hotel close by the port at this hour of the night. All the rooms were taken in anticipation of the ship's scheduled departure the next day. As they continued to look, they were approached by a young woman who told them that she knew of a room where they could stay if they needed a place. She was nicely dressed, attractive, and very pleasant. Out alone, talking to men this late at night, was not something a normal woman would be doing.

Guy and Ernesto knew exactly what she was offering them, and neither was interested in what she was pedaling. But they needed a room. As long as there was room for both of them, they would agree to go with her to check it out. She assured them there was room for two men. Michel would have to find a room on his own.

They followed her down a narrow side street to an old, but well-kept, hotel. She showed them a nicely furnished room with one large bed. She said they would have to sleep together in the one bed. The two men glanced at each other and agreed it would not be a problem for them. They were running out of options.

"How much for the room?" Guy asked.

"You'll have to pay me twenty-five francs for one night. And I will stay here with you."

Three in one bed? Both men rejected that idea and told her they would rather stay alone.

"Comme vous voudrez," she said. "Whatever you wish. It's going to cost the same whether I stay with you or not." She had not been used to such a blatant refusal, but since there were two of them anyway, she would find another place to spend the night.

"Let's pay the twenty-five francs and have her stay somewhere else," Ernesto suggested.

After paying her the money and assuring themselves that the room was securely locked, Guy and Ernesto settled into the room. It was already well past midnight, and they wouldn't get much sleep anyway, so they stayed up most of the night and talked about their situation and what they should do.

They would meet Michel at eight o'clock and tell him they did not want to go under these circumstances. They would then return to Paris.

Guy would have to somehow find a way to repay his cousin for the money Frank was about to lose.

SS. Paris *during its maiden voyage to New York in June 1921.*
The anchor chain is visible at the left front of the ship.

CHAPTER 5

The next morning, Guy and Ernesto went to the lobby, hoping to get some coffee. They may have grabbed a few hours of sleep during the short night—but if so, it wasn't much more than that. After the ordeal they experienced the previous evening, both were exhausted, physically and mentally. Fortunately, the hotel had a bar that also served food, and they casually helped themselves to some breakfast. By the time they finished, it was almost nine o'clock.

Michel had been waiting for them at their agreed-upon meeting point since eight o'clock. As the two men approached, they could see him walking angrily back and forth on the street, obviously not pleased that they were late.

"Why did you tell me last night that you would meet me at eight o'clock?" he asked.

He was concerned that they would miss their opportunity to get onto the ship.

However, the men were not at all worried about this, since they had already made what they thought was their final decision. They were going back to Paris. When did the train leave?

"No, we don't want to go anymore," they both said.

Michel refused to take no for an answer. He promised them it would be different this time, and they would like it much better this way.

"You'll get onto the boat like the other men working on the crew," he said. Guy and Ernesto had eliminated the idea of climbing up the anchor chain again but had to think about the possibility of boarding as part of the crew. Why hadn't they done it this way the first time? That would have prevented the distress they had already experienced.

The two men discussed it and decided that it might be worth another try as long as they didn't have to risk their lives again as they had done the previous night. If they failed to get onto the ship this time, all the authorities could do was deny them boarding—possibly call the harbor gendarme—and have them hauled off to jail for a few days. In either case, they would eventually make it back to Paris. What was there to lose? After much thought and deliberation, they reluctantly agreed that since they had come this far, it would be worth another try using a different, less risky method.

"Okay, we'll try it," Guy said. "But if we don't like it, we're going back to Paris."

Thinking ahead, they walked back to the hotel and asked the manager if that room was generally available or if that girl always had that room.

"Well, not every night, but once in a while, she brings someone here to spend the night," he admitted uncomfortably. The room would be available tonight. At least now, the two men had an idea of what they would do if Michel's new plan did not work out any better than the last one.

Michel had followed them to the hotel and was waiting outside. "You're going to have to change your clothes," he said. He showed them a suitcase with clothing inside that would be similar to those worn by the workers on the ship—not uniforms, but more informal work clothing. The nice suits they had worn leaving Paris were dirty and wrinkled from the anchor-climbing episode, but they would definitely stand out trying to get onto the ship as workers.

The men used the bathroom in the hotel lobby to change clothes. They stuffed the clothes they had been wearing back into the suitcase and handed it back to Michel.

"What if they catch us before we get onto the boat? We'll have to go back to Paris in these clothes?" they asked Michel.

It was the only good suit Guy had, the one he had worn to get here. Guy knew that a good suit like that cost about eight hundred francs (about $30 US at the time), and he didn't have that kind of money to just go out and buy a new one.

"Don't worry about the suitcase. You'll find it in your cabin on the ship," Michel assured them.

Cabin? As encouraging as that sounded, how would they get a cabin if they had no ticket, were dressed up as workers, and were about to be snuck onto the ship as stowaways? Wouldn't the other workers or anyone on the ship's staff notice they weren't supposed to be there? The whole idea seemed like a long shot.

Michel hailed a cab, and the three men drove the short distance to the harbor. They could see the SS *Paris* now parked at the dock. It was a huge ship with three black stacks. In the daylight, it appeared much larger than it looked the previous night in the dark. It had moved sometime during the night, after their frightful boarding attempt, and after the other ship they had seen parked there the previous night had departed. The anchor was retracted, and the ship was now tied to the dock with massive ropes.

Passengers were already boarding, carrying light day bags, using one of the ramps leading to the ship. Their heavy baggage and foot lockers had already been checked in to the workers on the dock who were using another ramp to load those bags and other cargo onto the ship. On the opposite side of the ramps, a small stand sold beer, hot dogs, and cola. A few dock workers stood in line to get lunch. Workers from the crew were returning to the ship, probably after having been out on the town. None were wearing suits.

Michel led them toward two French officers standing near the staff boarding ramp, dressed in fancy white uniforms. Very impressive, Guy thought. By the way they were dressed, these guys must be important. How could they be involved in this?

The officers exchanged greetings with Michel, who handed one of them a letter. Guy assumed it was the payment to bring Ernesto and him onboard. The officer studied the letter. He looked at the two men suspiciously as if he were checking their identity, then turned to Michel and shook hands with him, nodding that all was well. One of the officers then handed the two young men a small bag containing the uniforms that they would have to wear while on the ship. For now, they would pretend to be workers returning from a night out dressed in the civilian clothes they had been given earlier at the hotel. They had no idea what had happened to the suits they had worn on the train.

"This time, you'll make it to New York," Michel said confidently. "We'll see you there sometime."

Guy didn't know whether to take this as a pleasantry or a warning. Guy remembered Michel telling him on the train that he was a US citizen with an American passport, and that he was an Italian like them who had immigrated from Sicily. They didn't know whether Michel meant he would be on the ship with them, and he made no indication that he was returning to the United States anytime soon. Michel simply walked away and left them standing with the French officers.

One of the officers said to Guy and Ernesto in French, "You follow us. We are going to get on the boat now, and you stay a few feet behind us." They walked casually up the ramp toward the crew entrance of the ship.

The officers had assumed the young men also spoke French, having come from Paris. Fortunately, both men knew enough French that they understood.

They followed the officers up the ramp. However, when they reached the entrance, the officers paused before walking into the ship. They looked back and discreetly whispered to the two very tense men to relax, wait there a moment, have a cigarette, and act normally.

"Act like you belong here," one said.

Ernesto was a smoker, so for him it wasn't a problem to light up. In fact, it was a relief. Guy, on the other hand, did not smoke, and had never liked the habit. However, he tried to look like the others and lit a cigarette. As he inhaled, he immediately started to cough uncontrollably, and his eyes began to water. As hard as he tried, he could not stop the coughing. He looked at Ernesto and began to laugh and cough at the same time. His friend erupted into laughter as well, knowing that Guy was not a smoker and realizing the comic relief of the scene they were so seriously trying to create. The guard at the door saw Guy choking and joined in laughing as well. He assumed both men had too much to drink on shore and said nothing when they followed the two French officers into the entrance of the ship. Guy was pleasantly surprised and relieved that neither of the Italian men had to show passports or passes. Maybe this was going to work after all.

Once they were inside the ship, they waited for the ship's officers who had led them in. The officers had gone ahead of them so as to not raise any suspicions. When it was clear that Guy and Ernesto had made it into the ship, the two officers returned. They were joined by another crewmember dressed in work clothes, who led them through shiny hallways and dazzling staircases to the mid-level section of the boat.

Along the way, they saw what a luxurious ship the *Paris* really was. They passed a beautifully decorated bar and sitting lounge, a large, elegant dining room, a well-equipped gymnasium, and even a barbershop. Was this for first-class passengers? Whatever class it was, it was stunning, like out of a magazine. What would it be like to be able to travel in such style and not have to worry about hiding? They would never get to find out.

They were led to a vacant cabin. Signs on the floor indicated they were in second class, Deck C. The cabin was small but nicely furnished with bunk beds, carpet on the floor, and a vanity with a mirror and sink in the center. In one corner was a table with two small chairs, some shelves for luggage, and hooks for clothes. There was a small window, which allowed some natural light to penetrate the otherwise dark space. The room was an outside cabin.

One of the officers said to Guy, "You stay here on the floor under the bed and don't be afraid. I'll come to this cabin and move you." He handed Guy a blanket and told him to get under it.

The officer told Ernesto that he would have to go to another room. Neither man knew if they would see each other while on the boat, or whether they would spend the next week alone in hiding. Ernesto left the room with one of the officers and the other crew member. Would he ever see his friend again?

After a few minutes, the officer closed the cabin door but did not lock it. Guy was now alone, on the floor, uncomfortable, and very frightened. What if someone entered the room and found him hiding there under that blanket? Would that be the end of his journey? Certainly, this was not how he was going to travel to America. It couldn't be. Where were they going to move him? And when?

He lay there quietly and waited.

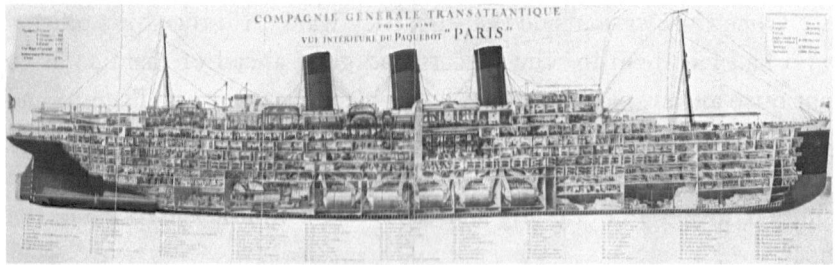

Interior Layout of SS Paris.

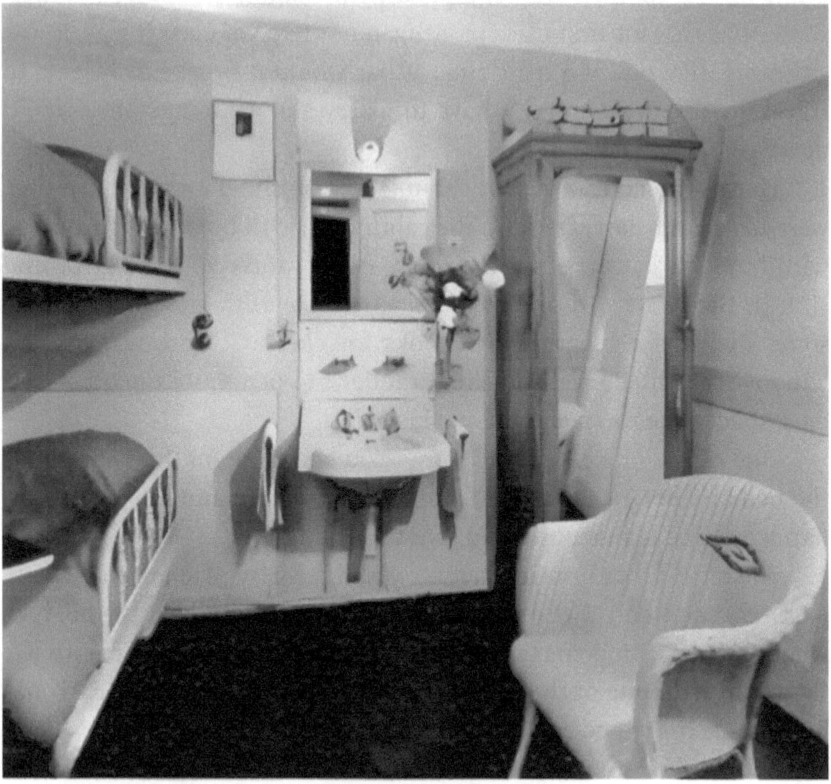

A Two Berth Cabin complete with a hot and cold water basin.

CHAPTER 6

Every minute seemed like a year to Guy under the blanket. He tossed and turned, trying to get comfortable on the floor. Every so often, he would look out from under the cover, but no one ever came into the room to check on him. By now, it had to be about eleven or twelve o'clock, and he knew that the ship was not supposed to leave Le Havre until five-thirty in the evening. He had no choice but to just lie there and wait.

As the hours crept slowly by, his muscles burned from cramping and his anxiety ballooned. He was not an overtly religious man, but he always had faith that God would see him through and that things would turn out as they were meant to. That faith had carried him as he left Italy to build a life in France, but his certainty was wavering now.

Less than twenty-four hours earlier, his biggest concerns were what he would have for dinner and where he would meet his friends that weekend. Now he was on his way to a new life in a new country yet again, this time on a ship—hiding out under the bed like a criminal. Had he made the right choice? Would he reach his destination, or would he be caught and sent back to France?

And if he somehow made it to America, would he ever be able to see his family back in Italy again? He had come to France five years ago seeking a better life, but he never intended to abandon his parents, brothers, sisters, and so many relatives and friends back home. He had planned to take a trip back as soon as he had saved enough and to bring them money to help out on the farm. He had no way of knowing it then, but that trip back wouldn't happen for another twenty years.

Abruptly, he felt the ship move. Banging, bumping, and muffled horn blasts accompanied their departure. It must be after five, he thought. He had been lying there for six hours.

There was still no activity in the cabin. Nobody had come in, and there were no suitcases left in the room, so maybe no one was going to use this cabin after all. Guy's sense of time was dilated from spending so long under the blanket, but after what he guessed was about twenty minutes, he heard voices outside the cabin door. Two sets of feet entered the room. When he heard the door open, Guy hesitantly peered out from under the blanket and saw a man staring back at him. His mind was still in a daze, and he wasn't sure who the man was. He thought for sure he had been caught.

Then he saw the other man who had also entered the cabin and realized with palpable relief that it was one of the crew members who had brought him there. They signaled all was safe now, and he could at last come out from under the blanket and get off the floor. Guy stood up cautiously, feeling the blood finally circulating through his legs again. He peered out the small window and could see they were moving through the water.

"We think this cabin is now yours until we reach New York," said the man he recognized. "But do not get into the bed until we leave London. The ship is going to stop, and there might be some passengers who have booked this cabin. If so, we'll come for you before they come aboard, and we'll take you to another place. Just stay in the room, but don't get into the bed. If someone does come in, just tell them you're a crewmember hiding out to take a short nap."

It took about an hour and a half to reach England. The sound of the four steam-powered turbine propellers changed into a low-pitched hum and eventually stopped altogether. As he looked out the window, he could see the ship had anchored out in the ocean, just as it had been when Guy first saw it the previous evening. They had reached Plymouth, the stopping point just outside of London where more passengers would board for New York.

The stopover was short, perhaps two hours. Through the window,

Guy watched several small boats bringing passengers from shore to the anchored ship. People walked by noisily in the hallways, bags bumping the walls, as they found their cabins. But no one attempted to enter his. Maybe he would be safe and able to stay right here.

The engines came to life, the massive propellers roared, and the ship moved again. They were on their way to New York! After a short while, the same crew member who had told him not to use the bed entered the room.

"Nobody is coming," he said. "This will be your cabin until we get to New York. Now you can sleep in the bed and use all the things in this room—the towels, writing paper, and the cabinets."

Guy hadn't dared to imagine such comfort as he was climbing the anchor chain last night. But now relief washed over him again as he realized he would spend the rest of this trip in a cabin, and as a normal person, rather than as an animal on the floor. He was safe, at least for now. He had not even thought about what was about to happen once he arrived in New York beyond assuming Frank would be there waiting for him.

The door opened again, and another crew member came into the cabin along with Ernesto, who was carrying the suitcase of their belongings that Michel had promised would make it onto the ship. When Guy and Ernesto saw each other, they laughed in disbelief . . . They had made it this far, much farther than they could have imagined, and were glad to see each other. They embraced.

Ernesto asked, "Were you in this room the entire time?"

"Yes, I was here hiding under a blanket beneath the bed. Where did they put you?"

"Guy, you had it nice in here! You should have seen where they put me! That place was more like a tiny storage area in the engine room, with no bed, nothing there. I had to squeeze my body just to get in. Once I was inside, I had no idea how I was ever going to get out. The hole was that tight. Compared to me, you had it good!"

The crew member in the cabin listened intently to their lively discussion, and he seemed keenly interested in their situation. He explained to them he was a cook in the second-class kitchen and would take care of providing them food every day. This was becoming too good to be true.

"Just stay here in the cabin and don't go around the ship or up the stairs," he advised.

He left but soon returned with food, wine, and cigarettes. Guy and Ernesto relaxed at the small table in a corner of the cabin and enjoyed a delicious meal with a bottle of good French wine. They had been on this journey for only a day and a half, but it seemed so much longer since they had left Paris. Now that they had left Plymouth and were sailing directly to New York, they had six more days to go.

The other crew member—the one Guy had first seen from under the blanket—came by the next day and introduced himself . . . It appeared that both the kitchen manager and the cook were participants in the stowaway scheme, though neither man offered details and Guy didn't ask questions.

Though Guy and Ernesto hadn't seen the two officers who escorted them onboard since they were brought to the cabin, these other two crew members became very friendly.

Each night, about an hour after the passengers were served in the second-class dining room, the crew members would come to the cabin with food, along with the best cheeses, wine, and dessert for Guy and Ernesto. Later, after their duties in the kitchen were over, both would return and stay for drinks, conversation, and companionship. Good company wasn't the only draw for the crew; this second-class stateroom was much more comfortable and spacious than the cramped crew quarters they were accustomed to living in.

Guy hadn't eaten this well in years. He felt as if he were a full-paying passenger, not a mere stowaway. Hopefully, Frank was getting his money's worth. He couldn't wait to see him and tell him all about it. Other than the boredom of having to stay inside the cabin, he was actually enjoying this trip.

But the joy and contentment were about to end as soon as the ship arrived in New York. He just didn't know it yet.

CHAPTER 7

Living the life of a passenger in second class aboard the SS *Paris* bound for New York City was an experience Guy had never imagined he would have, even if he couldn't leave the cabin. Maybe one day he would save enough to buy a real ticket on a ship. A second-class ticket to New York on a ship in 1929 cost about $600 (equivalent to over $10,000 in 2023), more than Guy could earn in a year. If he ever did buy a real ticket, he thought, it would certainly be in third class—nothing like this. He had to keep reminding himself that he was still a stowaway. He could easily be caught at any time—arrested, jailed, and sent back. For now, cabin life was good.

"When do we have to do something, or act like we work on the ship?" Guy asked one of the crew members while they were having dinner together one night.

"Not until we get to New York. We'll come for you and let you know what you'll have to do. That's why you have the work clothes we gave you. For now, you don't have to do anything. Just don't leave the cabin."

Ernesto and Guy spent the time talking and resting. Guy realized that the last two days had not only been mentally exhausting but had also taken quite a physical toll on him. He needed the rest.

He spent some of the time reading; there were brochures about the ship in the room, and their new friends on the crew brought them a newspaper. There was also stationery available, so Guy began writing letters. He had no idea if or when he would get to mail them once they reached New York, but it gave him something to do.

He had to let his parents know he was on his way to New York and would soon be with Frank. Promising to write more when he got there and when he had an address for them to respond to, he left out most of the details, not wanting them to worry.

While his journey away from his family had just taken a sudden and drastic turn, it had begun many years earlier. The thought of them and his family back in Italy brought a wave of sadness over him. He had been gone five years already. They had been close, and he missed them terribly. When would he see them again? Would he ever?

He had always enjoyed the beauty of the land and closeness of his many friends and family, even though his youth had been difficult. His mother had died twenty days after his birth, and his father had given him to another woman to raise until he was two years old. His father remarried and went on to have five more children with his stepmother.

Like most of his friends, Guy had to drop out of the one-room schoolhouse in his neighborhood after the fourth grade. Fortunately, he was a bright child and had learned to read and write Italian by then. However, most of his young life in Italy was spent as a *contadino*, growing fruit and vegetables and raising animals on the family farm, as was dictated by the fundamental and sacred Italian tradition of *l'ordine della famiglia*. This unwritten but all-encompassing set of expectations around family hierarchy, behavior, and allegiance controlled how you were to act within the family structure and how you were to react to influences outside of it.

This family system stipulated that unmarried sons would contribute to the support of their parents and siblings by living at home and working on the farm. Any money earned working outside the farm—Guy also worked as a laborer for the railroad to earn extra for his family—was to be given to his mother, just as his father would do. In the old Italian way—*la via vecchia*—the father may have been the head of the family, but the mother was the center. While his father was responsible for the general welfare of his family, the mother was responsible for the management of the household, collecting any money that was brought in, and for controlling the budget of the family. Sons were expected to support the family, both physically and socially, and to defend their family's and sisters' honor.

The first time Guy left home was in 1921, at age nineteen, when the army called him into service. All young men in Italy had to serve time in the military. Fortunately, Guy had been too young to be called into combat in World War I and so escaped being one of the 600,000 Italians killed or 950,000 Italians wounded by that conflict.

The army sent him to Cremona, a picturesque town near Milan, where he served his military obligation for thirteen months. Cremona was an ancient city, founded by the Romans in 218 BC, which grew into one of the largest towns in Northern Italy. Lying in the Po Valley, it was on the main road across the country, called the Via Postuma, which was used to supply troops to Julius Caesar during his military campaigns. Over the centuries, Cremona had become renowned as a cultural hub and the center of musical instrument manufacture in Italy, most notably the Guarneri and Stradivari workshops. All of that history, art, and music had such an impact on Guy that as soon as he returned home from the army, he couldn't wait to leave again.

This itch was exacerbated by the fact that when he arrived back home, the few jobs available to him were low-paying and required long hours of difficult manual labor. Northern Italy had advanced over the years in culture, wealth, architecture, and living conditions. But the provinces south and east of Rome, where Guy was from, had stagnated and become known as the *Mezzogiorno*, also called "the land that time forgot."

In that area of Italy, there was no electricity. There were no lights, just candles or kerosene. When the sun went down, it got dark—and stayed that way until sunrise. While Guy was in Cremona, he had seen the big city and bright lights—that was how he wanted to live. Had he not gone into the army and seen another way of life, he might have stayed home on the farm, and his life may have been vastly different.

For a little while, he tried to bring that brightness home: he briefly worked in a neighboring town, San Giovanni Incarico, on a hydroelectric dam on the Liri River that would produce electricity for the area. But when an opportunity came to experience the lights and culture of the city again, he seized it. His friend, Eleuterio, also from Arce, worked at a factory in France and had written to Guy telling him that his company was looking for workers and he should come. After communicating by mail with his friend and the owners of the factory, he received the official documentation he would need to cross the border into France. He had to sign a written contract and agree to work there for at least one year, but he felt it was worth it.

Telling his parents that he wanted to leave the farm, and Italy altogether, was difficult. Naturally, they were upset, didn't want him to go, and tried hard to talk him out of it. They would be losing a son and a strong worker. But Guy saw no way to build a good life for himself at home. He was determined to step out of *l'ordine della famiglia* and do it his way—with an appetite for more and a risk-taking attitude that would guide him in future life-altering decisions too.

"You know, Daddy, I'll come back in six months," he said at the time. Even though his contract in France was for a year, he was hoping he would be able to visit at least once.

Whether Guy really believed that would happen was something he never talked about and wouldn't know until he had experienced life away from them and the farm.

He traveled by train to a town called Saint-Galmier, with a population of about 2,500. It was not far from the Italian border, close to the big city of Lyon, and about five hundred miles south of Paris. Located on the river Coise, Saint-Galmier was famous for the production of a well-known brand of carbonated mineral water called Badoit.

The French had used the thermal springs in this area for their therapeutic qualities as far back as the eighteenth century. In 1837, Auguste Badoit acquired the lease on one of the springs and ran it as a spa. He began bottling the water a year later, and after ten years, he closed the spa and concentrated on marketing sparkling water. By the time he died in 1858, 1.5 million bottles of Badoit water were being sold each year. In 1883, the business expanded by buying a glass factory and producing its own bottles. Guy would be working at the glass factory making bottles.

Eleuterio was waiting for him at the train station, took him to dinner, and filled him in on what to expect on the job and what life was like in Saint-Galmier. The year was 1924. This was Guy's first time out of Italy, and at age twenty-two, he was excited to begin a new life.

His job in the bottling plant involved taking the glass molds out of the hot oven with tongs, placing them on the conveyer belt so that they would cool and then inserting the bottles into boxes. He worked a different schedule each week, as the plant operated twenty-four hours a day. Sometimes he even would work Saturdays for overtime, loading those boxes into trucks. He earned about a dollar a day, but since the company provided shared housing, even at that wage, he was able to save money.

Life was good—and electrically illuminated—for Gaetano, a refreshing change from the dark, dreary life he had left behind in Italy. He did his job well, and it was easier than being on the farm in Italy, where he worked hard and was always tired. Guy also liked being able to go fishing in the river Coise, a tributary of the Loire, which flows through the town. He was happy in France.

He learned to speak and read French. The town was beautiful, and the people were very friendly. He would have renewed his contract and stayed there, but soon, he began to experience ill effects from the health hazards of the bottle-making process. His eyes were often red and watery, and his stomach started to swell due to the chemicals used to make glass, particularly foul-smelling sulfur. He saw a lot of other people suffering as well.

After his one-year obligatory contract was over, he told his boss he was leaving. When he explained the reasons why, he was offered a job doing something else in the factory where he would be less exposed to the chemicals. He was a good worker, and the company wanted him to stay. However, he had already received letters from Italian friends in Paris who told him about the many opportunities to work there. They promised he would have a job if he came to Paris.

Living in Paris was so appealing to him that he told his boss the decision had been made. He packed the few belongings he had accumulated in Saint-Galmier, said good-bye to his friends, and took the train north to Paris. A new life awaited the twenty-three-year-old, but he had no idea what it would be like or what to expect. He was willing to try something new and to experience the next adventure on his journey, just as he had done by leaving home.

The house in Arce, Italy, where Guy was born in 1902.

The cornerstone of the house showing the year built as 1697.

View of the Main Street (Corso) in Arce around 1900.

View of the town of Arce, Italy, in 2023.

Church in Arce where Guy was baptized in 1902 as it appeared in 1914.

Church of the Apostles Saint Peter and Paul in 2023.

Gaetano as a 20-year-old soldier in 1922 in Cremona, Italy.

Day pass issued to Guy for off-base activity dated 19 Oct, 1922, at army base in Cremona.

Above and below: The hydroelectric dam at San Giovanni Incarico
where Guy worked upon returning from the army in 1924.

Badoit Factory built in 1897 as seen in 2023.

Gaetano's first job at Badoit in Saint-Galmier, France (1924-1925).

Badoit
1778

A City That Sparkles
Badoit's natural mineral water makes the village of Saint-Galmier
sparkle with joy, where its spring springs up.

Badoit protects!
For preserving nature around its source and purity of its water for
future generations, Badoit co-created the La Bulle Verte association
in 2010 with local communities and supports local farmers.

Find out how on www.badoit.fr

Label from bottle of Badoit Sparkling Water, 2024.

CHAPTER 8

Paris was as wonderful as he had hoped it would be. In fact, it was beyond anything that he could imagine coming from such a simple life in Italy. It was so visually exciting and mentally exhilarating compared to the year he had spent in Saint-Galmier. As nice as that small town was, it was not anything like Paris.

During the 1920s, Paris was changing from a traditional post-war European city to a modern, risqué, unconventional one. The jazz scene had taken hold in dance halls and nightclubs, and people were swinging until the early morning. Social and sexual norms for women—even for men—were becoming more liberal and adventurous.

Guy witnessed these changes with amazement, but as an Italian laborer living in Paris he did not participate. Even if he could have afforded that lifestyle, he would not have chosen it. He was bold enough to chase a better life, but the glamorous, modern style didn't fit him. He stayed close to his friends living in the Italian suburbs of Paris and embraced the familiar Italian culture.

Occasionally he explored the Left Bank or would cross the river to Montmartre, where the shops, coffeehouses, and bars were less expensive, and he and his friends could enjoy a more affordable night out together. The French franc had been devalued in the 1920s, so his wages went much further than they would have before the war. He saved quite a bit from his salary, since his room, board, and other expenses were exceptionally low. The more he saved and the longer he stayed in France, the more he was able to accumulate in his bank account.

Prohibition had become law in America, so Paris became a popular destination for international tourism, especially for Americans. The thought of going to America someday had always intrigued Guy. His cousin Frank and several friends had gone over during the period of mass migration to America, when four million Italians arrived in the United States. Even Guy's father, Antonio, had tried life in America, sailing over on the White Star Line's SS *Canopic* to Boston in 1910 during the height of the immigration wave between 1900 and 1914.

Many of these immigrants, like Guy's father, stayed only a few years, earned as much money as they could, and then went back to their lives and families in the old country. Antonio had gone to New York, found work in Maine for two years, and returned to Italy when Guy was ten years old. He could not remember whether his father had left Italy planning to return—as did many of them—or whether his father had found the living and working conditions in America, especially in Maine, too difficult.

Cousin Frank and a few friends had stayed. Every so often, Guy would write to them, and they would tell him about life in America. Many of the stories were not good, even though he knew they often left out the full details of their harsh living conditions so as not to discourage others.

Despite the hardships, life in America still appealed to Guy. But he had basically given up that dream because of the new restrictions, aimed to lower the number of unskilled workers who had been pouring into the country up to that point, providing the labor pool from which the country's infrastructure would be built.

His primary job in Paris was to operate a crane that lifted cement from the ground to the floors of buildings under construction. The system of pumping cement to each floor had not yet been perfected. If his load was steel or cement blocks, it was simply a matter of lifting those supplies to the required floor. If it was wet cement, the slurry was placed in a container on wheels before Guy lifted the cart to the right floor and guided it onto rails laid on the floor that would take it to the desired location. Using a series of audible rings as signals, Guy listened to the number of rings from the men on the receiving end and operated the crane up or down based on those signals. The work required focus and coordination but little of the hard manual labor he was used to doing in Italy.

He worked every weekday and often on Saturdays. It was a good job—it paid well, and he enjoyed it. He was making five and a half francs an hour or about twenty-one cents ($3.60/hour adjusted for inflation in 2023), a good hourly rate at that time for construction jobs in France and fifty percent more than he had been earning in Saint-Galmier. On some weekends, he would earn another twenty or thirty francs (about one dollar US per day) working for another company on the side when they needed him to lift some of their building materials.

He belonged to a large Italian community of *paisanos* living in Paris, many from his hometown in Italy, so he had an active social life. He met a girl named Marie who lived in an Italian neighborhood of Paris called Vitry-sur-Seine. Her father owned a building, which housed a grocery store, a small French bistro, and a liquor store. Guy would often ride his bicycle there to see a friend who introduced him to Marie, a waitress in the restaurant. She and her family lived in the apartment on the second floor of the building.

He met resistance right away from the girl's mother and father, who didn't want their daughter involved with a man so much older. Marie was only sixteen years old, and Guy was twenty-seven. They thought he was a nice enough fellow, but the age difference was too much for them. Even though Marie was from an Italian family that had come from a town in Italy not far from where Guy had grown up, they didn't trust him or his motives.

He talked to Marie's mother and father and asked them if he and Marie could go out together. They reluctantly agreed, but only if their niece accompanied them on these dates. They would go to the movies or to dances, and their niece would be present. Eventually, the niece would leave them alone and go off on her own. Then she would meet them again somewhere before the night was over to escort the couple home. It was a strange arrangement, but Guy liked Marie and could tell she felt the same way about him. He looked forward to them getting to know each other better. He had dated lots of girls since his army days, but this was his first serious girlfriend.

And now what had he done? All of a sudden he had thrown away the chance at a lasting relationship with Marie—and the good life he had built in Paris. Guy was about to enter a new world—a new life—one that he had not been prepared for, one he did not expect. He sat in the cabin and tried to explain it all to Marie in a letter, though it was difficult to find the words. Would she even believe it, even though he was writing the tale on SS *Paris* stationery?

After all, it was difficult enough for him to believe it was actually happening.

The house in Paris where Guy and Marie met in 1928 as it appears in 2024.

CHAPTER 9

Every so often, Guy and Ernesto heard voices or a commotion in the hall. Each time, they froze, held their breath, and nervously waited for the door to be flung open and their covert presence to be uncovered. Should they crawl under the bed? Pretend to be asleep? If they were, in fact, discovered, should they expose the crew members involved in the scheme? The fear racked Guy's mind.

But the only time the door opened was by their own hand, carefully unlocked after their kitchen friends knocked and identified themselves. Always vigilant that there might be others who had discovered the truth, Guy and Ernesto could never be sure that maybe this time other crew members would accompany their friends to apprehend the stowaways. There was nothing they could do to prevent this from happening, but the anxiety was always there whenever they heard voices in the hallway or knocks on the door.

With little else to do but think all day, Guy wondered whether he and Ernesto were the only stowaways on the ship. It would not surprise him if there were others. But where were they? Were there any who had secretly slipped aboard on their own? Guy remembered hearing stories of friends from his hometown in Italy who had tried it. All of them had been caught and sent back to Italy.

Stowing away was more common than Guy even knew. Being a stowaway became a popular fad for several years, with the peak of the trend occurring around 1927 and 1928, just before Guy and Ernesto's adventure in 1929. In those two years alone, it was estimated that more than five hundred people were able to slip aboard ships destined for the United States. At the time, many magazine articles and newspaper stories glamorized those who succeeded.

In 1928, a nineteen-year-old German man attempted to sneak across from Hamburg to New York by nailing himself into a long shipping box filled with food and provisions and marked as household goods. As the box was being unloaded from the ship in New York, the erratic movements jolted him loose from his secure rigging inside the box and caused him to cry out. He was discovered by a dockworker. But because of the notoriety he received in the newspapers, not only did the "Coffin Stowaway" become a celebrity, but he was also offered a job and allowed to remain in America.

Most others were not as fortunate. Shortly after the episode of the young German, an adventurous Italian who was constructing the interior woodworking of the new Italian ocean liner SS *Conte Grande* built himself a secret room above the first-class dining area. He furnished it with an electric light, reading material, a cot, and a chair, along with water, wine, bread, salami, and fruit, and snuck into this little haven before the ship's departure. However, he foolishly began wandering about the ship during the voyage and was discovered and detained by a crew member. Upon arrival at Ellis Island, despite the interest and attention he received from the press, he was deported and faced arrest in Italy.

By the time of Guy's journey, newspapers had stopped glamorizing stowaways and were writing stories about the darker side of the issue. Headline stories described people being crushed to death in baggage holds of ships, roasted alive in boiler rooms, or frozen to death hiding in lifeboats.

The outcome for most stowaways if they survived the trip—as it had been for Guy's friends—was to be caught and deported from Ellis Island back to their home country. Guy knew this and feared he would meet the same fate, but he also knew he hadn't made the attempt entirely alone. He didn't know what he had been caught up in, only that his cousin Frank would be waiting for him in New York and that might increase his chances of being able to stay if he wasn't caught first.

Not all immigrants were stowaways, of course. One type of

scheme that had been used to entice poor Italians to make the journey to America was called the *padrone* system. It was used extensively during the height of the immigration movement in the late 1800s and early 1900s. Guy had heard of people from his region who had gone to America this way, but his situation didn't seem to quite fit that model, either.

Under the *padrone* system, poor Italians—and other would-be emigrants wanting to go to the United States—were approached by agents, many of whom worked for the shipping lines themselves or for American businesses needing labor. These agents would lure these unsuspecting people by offering them small amounts of money as loans, which they could use to purchase a ticket to America. In return, they would agree to work for some American company or labor boss (*padrone*) for a set time period, often at extremely low wages and with exorbitant interest rates and conditions to repay the loan.

These agents would promise them passage on a ship to America, a job, and a place to stay when they arrived. The ticket they were given meant they were not stowaways. The passage, however, was in steerage class—in the belly of the ship—where living conditions were unbearable, food was scarce and barely edible, and sanitary provisions were substandard or nonexistent.

Emigrants not only became seasick, but many also developed horrible diseases like typhus, dysentery, cholera, pneumonia, and smallpox that spread quickly in the squalid, crowded surroundings, even if they had been perfectly healthy when they boarded the ship. The lack of clean drinking water, the rancid food, and being forced to stay below and use buckets to relieve themselves during stormy conditions—the only bathrooms were located above deck—made this trip a nightmare for most, especially for older people and children. Some died and had to be buried at sea.

Conditions improved somewhat during the latter part of the nineteenth century due to stricter maritime laws aimed at regulating transatlantic travel, and newer, faster ships. However, the journey in steerage class was still fraught with suffering. The jobs awaiting the contracted laborers were often not what was promised, or were located in remote areas of the country, or required difficult and demeaning manual labor. The lodging promised by the *padrone* was also often substandard—groups of men or entire families packed together like cattle in a one-room boarding house.

The wages they earned were extremely low. Italian immigrants were at the bottom of the economic ladder. A report by the US Immigration Commission in 1910 stated that, while the national average wage that year was $666, Italian immigrants earned an average of $396 per year—less than African Americans, who were earning an average of $445. Italians were often used as scabs to break strikes at coal mines or at railroads in the Midwest. They were often made to pay a *bossatura*, an under-the-table job tax.

While it cost thirty to forty dollars at the time to travel in steerage, it was a lot of money for these poor Italians. It amounted to roughly one hundred days of wages to an average Southern Italian *contadino*. Since many found it difficult to obtain farm work for even one hundred days, it often represented a year's wages for one of them. Traveling with wives, children, parents, and even grandparents, the cost of going to America was staggering. If they were fortunate to have saved enough to buy a ticket on their own, they would still be required to pay for food, lodging, and other incidental travel expenses just to get to the ship's departure point. There was usually nothing left by the time the family arrived in America.

If a *padrone* were involved, it would take years for them to pay the loan back.

Most of the people who chose to migrate to America weren't aware of the financial realities that awaited them in the "promised land." Even if they had known, they would agree that it would still be better than the life they faced in Italy. They risked leaving their homes, relatives, friends—all they had—to come to America, whether under a *padrone* or through some meager savings they had been able to acquire on their own. The Italians had a name for the kind of life they would otherwise endure if they stayed in Southern Italy—*la miseria*—a life of poverty, destitution, and misery.

Unfortunately, many people making the arduous voyage from Italy specifically to avoid such a life of misery became victims of similar horrors and living conditions once they arrived in America, even if they didn't come via the *padrone* system. Prior to 1855, there was no immigration control. Weary, unknowing immigrants were simply allowed to exit the ship and walk into America. They immediately fell prey to all sorts of crooks and swindlers who offered false promises of great jobs, housing, or cheap passage to other parts of the country. No matter what, these poor immigrants were forced to pay what they had agreed to.

In 1855, a landing station at an old fort in New York called Castle Garden was established to act as more of a clearing house where people who weren't able to speak English could receive legitimate assistance from social services, travel agencies, and employment offices. But soon the country became overwhelmed with immigrants and needed a way to screen the newcomers. Many had no money, no relatives, or no potential livelihood. Others brought in serious medical conditions or diseases and would likely become a "burden" to the United States.

In 1892, Ellis Island became the inspection center immigrants had to clear before being allowed to enter the United States. The Italians referred to it as the *isola della lacrime*—the island of tears—because about 2 percent of the new arrivals were refused entry by uniformed officers and sent back home. Families were often forced to make the decision to split up if one or more failed to pass inspection. Going back home meant returning to a life of complete destitution, as most of these families had sold all they had just to afford the journey.

In the early 1900s, a hospital on Ellis Island was established to treat those immigrants with contagious diseases before allowing them entry into the country. It also treated patients with dangerous physical and mental conditions to get them healthy enough to make the return trip home if they had been rejected. Some of its methods were controversial. Accusations included the use of eugenics to exclude people and groups judged to be genetically inferior. People from Southern Italy were often included in this group.

In 1914, the year the complex was completed, over 10,000 patients from seventy-five countries were treated at the hospital and many were then allowed to enter the United States. While 350 babies were born on Ellis Island, there were also approximately 3,500 deaths.

Even though they were traveling in steerage class, the names, dates of birth, and hometowns of immigrants brought over by the *padroni* were listed on the ship's manifest, the same as the other passengers who had paid to have cabins on the ship. As deceitful and dishonest as the *padrone* system was, it offered these desperate migrants a legal way to enter the United States. They were processed and cleared at Ellis Island just like those who had managed to pay their own way. The *padrone* had warned them in advance not to admit to signing any type of labor contract or obligation. If they did, they would be rejected and sent back. If they managed to clear the confusing immigration process, including the humiliating medical probes and examinations, they were allowed to enter.

They were not considered stowaways.

But Guy and Ernesto were not listed on the ship's manifest like the other passengers. While someone had supposedly paid for their voyage—Frank, in this case—Guy and Ernesto were not supposed to be on that ship.

They were illegal stowaways and would not be going through Ellis Island to get into America.

CHAPTER 10

It was March 12, 1929, and the ship had left Le Havre just six days before. Finally, the day they had been waiting for had arrived. After six days at sea, the ship was about to dock in New York Harbor. They were thankful for the comforts they were able to enjoy on the voyage—they knew that it could have been a lot worse.

As a result of tighter immigration restrictions, reduced travel demand, and the outcry from government and passengers alike about its foul conditions, steerage class had already been eliminated on most ships. But there was also third class, or "tourist" class, a less costly alternative to traveling in second class. While a cabin in third class would have been fine with Guy, it would not have been nearly as comfortable and enjoyable. It would certainly be better than having to hide in the boiler room or in a lifeboat!

Thanks to their new friends in the kitchen, they had eaten as well as they could remember. The seas had been calm with no severe storms en route, so they enjoyed a smooth ride the entire way. Their days had passed with a mix of trepidation, fear, and excitement—imagining what this world would hold for them.

Guy wondered if he would live in the "Little Italy" section of Boston that he had heard so much about from his cousin. Called the North End, it included several blocks of Italian tenements and hundreds of small food and drinking establishments, bakeries, and outdoor fruit, vegetable, meat, and fish markets.

His cousin Frank lived in Newton, a suburb of Boston. It was a residential area made up of thirteen small neighborhood villages, many of them Italian enclaves with sections of *paisanos* from the same town or area in Italy. Frank had written to him about the town, its numerous Italian restaurants, grocery stores, churches, and parks with soccer fields and *bocce ball* courts. It sounded wonderful. Maybe that's where he would live, he thought. His cousin was there with his family and friends. Guy would even know some of the people there who Frank had mentioned in his letters, since many had immigrated to Boston years earlier from his hometown in Italy.

For the twenty-four-year-old Ernesto, this immigration attempt had to work. He believed the third time would be a charm for him. So far, it was proceeding much better than he expected—certainly better than his first two tries as a stowaway. It was difficult to believe he was doing it again, and that he made the decision so suddenly. He was determined to get to America, knowing the obstacles he would face and that his brother in Detroit had no idea he was coming. The first time, when he was only twelve years old, he was caught alone on the ship as it was arriving in New York and was sent back to Italy. It had been a frightening experience, but it did not deter him.

He tried again several years later as a teenager, thinking he knew how to game the system better. Unlike his first attempt, which was from Italy, this attempt had been after he had already moved to Paris from his home in Sora, Italy, only ten miles from Guy's hometown of Arce.

That part of Italy is home to historic old towns nestled on picturesque hilltops with views extending hundreds of miles in all directions. In the fertile river valleys that meander below these villages, the landscape now abounds with gardens of lush vegetables, orchards of grape vines, and groves of olive trees.

This fascinating part of Italy would later be referred to as Ciociaria. The name was derived from the *ciocia*, a type of footwear worn by many of its poor inhabitants. Made with large leather soles, tied to the leg by straps around the ankle and knee, their use became so widespread, the peasants were called *ciociari* ("ciocia-wearers"), an often derogatory dialectal word referring to poor, unsophisticated country folk. Now it is embraced as an important part of the folklore of the region.

With a vast richness of history, culture, and beauty, it was still a land of scarcity. This is what Guy and Ernesto experienced as young boys in the early 1900s. Food was difficult to grow, there was no plumbing, and little access to clean water. To get to the few natural springs—*the fontanella*—Guy and his family walked several miles—sometimes daily—just to wash, do their laundry, or fill huge containers with drinking water to carry home for themselves, their thirsty animals, or their gardens.

While Northern Italy prospered in the post-unification period, Ciociaria, and most of Southern Italy, was marginalized and left behind by the power brokers of the new country. Promises made to the region by the new government authorities were ignored or broken. Distrust of the government and rebellion against the new order continued to prevail. The economy of Southern Italy was left to collapse. Both Guy and Ernesto had escaped *la miseria* for the same reasons—abject poverty, constant hunger, no jobs—initially finding better opportunities in France—and both now shared the hope of a new and even better life in America.

The second attempt to stow away to America did not end well for Ernesto. He was discovered on the ship at Le Havre soon after departure before the ship fully left the harbor. Despite his desperate pleas, the crew members who captured him threw him overboard a short distance from the dock. He could not swim. If it were not for some fishermen nearby who pulled him out of the icy waters, that attempt would have been his last.

Would he make it to Detroit this time?

They were not going to take any chances on this trip. Not once did they leave their cabin to explore the ship or dare go up on deck to get some fresh air. As anxious as they were to get out of their cabin and off the ship, they were frightened by the thought of what would happen if they were caught.

They had not been told any details of how they were going to get off the ship, only that at a certain time, they would change into the work clothes they were provided when they boarded and would be led out into the other parts of the ship, where they would pose as members of the crew, acting as if they belonged there.

Their job would be to clean and polish the brass handrails,

doorknobs, and other metal furnishings in the hallways of the ship. As the government inspectors came through looking for contraband, especially liquor—and for stowaways—the hope was they would go unnoticed. There would be other crew members performing the same work, so the inspectors would assume that Guy and Ernesto were just part of the crew.

What would happen to them after that was still a mystery.

Guy felt the ship slow for its arrival in New York. The sound of the diesel engines changed to a low roar. As he peered out the small cabin window, he could see nothing. He heard the sound of passengers in the hallway, proceeding excitedly to the deck to get a glimpse of the Statue of Liberty as they sailed through the narrow straits of the Verrazzano channel between Brooklyn and Staten Island. It was early in the morning and still dark outside. Guy and Ernesto had to stay hidden in their cabin. They did not get to see Lady Liberty like everyone else. They were on the wrong side of the ship.

As the ship approached Pier 57 on the west side of Manhattan near 14th Street in the Chelsea section of New York, they heard noises in the hallway that became louder and more frequent. Crew members called out orders and scurried around, getting ready for arrival. It sounded to Guy as if passengers were also passing by in the hallway, heading for the debarkation doors. Since they were in the second-class section, these passengers and those in first class—unlike those in third—would not have to get on the small boats to Ellis Island. They would undergo a cursory immigration inspection getting off the ship and, unless there was a major issue or obvious medical problem, these passengers would be free to enter the United States directly from the dock.

Suddenly, there was a knock. Guy unlocked the door, and the two friendly crew members barged into the cabin. Only now, they didn't appear so friendly. As they took quick nervous glances at each other, Guy could see the sweat on their skin and the tightness in their jaws.

Their calm demeanor from the night before—as they casually discussed what Guy and Ernesto would have to do while they shared a bottle of wine—had turned into a worried, serious tone. It was obvious to Guy that a critical moment had arrived for these crew members, who knew they would also be in serious trouble if the stowaways in their charge were caught now.

"Get changed. It's time," one of them said.

When they were ready, the men handed Guy and Ernesto some polishing cloths and cream. As passengers continued streaming through the halls and down the stairs, Guy and Ernesto were to shine the railings.

"Be cautious, but do not appear apprehensive," they were told.

Now that they had officially arrived in America, the customs officials would inspect the boat. They would check every room looking for liquor—or anything else that had been brought in illegally.

Including them.

Map of Ciociaria area of Italy.

CHAPTER 11

As they ventured out into the hallway from the safety of their cabin, Guy suddenly felt exposed, and the fear of being caught momentarily overcame him. He paused. Had he come all this way to now be caught and sent back? He didn't want to even think about the other alternatives.

He forced himself to act normally and began to work as he had been instructed. There were still people passing him in the halls, but most of the passengers had already gone to their designated exits, where they would be directed to the baggage claim areas. Guy worked one side of the hallway and Ernesto the other, both trying to stay inconspicuous, but close enough that they could see each other. Catching each other's eye, their shared disbelief, nervousness, and hope erupted as laughter just as an inspector walked swiftly by in a pressed uniform. But he kept going.

"Don't look at me," Guy told his friend, looking down and focusing hard on his hands as he polished. Other crew members were also working, cleaning rooms, or doing the same as they were. More inspectors passed by, and nothing seemed unusual.

This might be a good time to see the inside of the ship, Guy thought.

Occasionally, a uniformed inspector would come by or look through one of the rooms nearby. However, no one paid any attention to Guy or Ernesto.

So far, the masquerade was working.

As they made their way along Deck C, shining whatever they could, they could see some of the other rooms around the enormous ship. Their cabin was located toward the rear, and as they worked forward, they passed other second-class cabins that were the same as theirs. The doors were left open, awaiting the cleaning crew to change the linens and ready the room for the departure back to France. The SS *Paris* was scheduled to leave again in a few days.

From the hall they could see the second-class dining room. It looked as if it seated hundreds at a time. Guy assumed this was the area where their friends had worked to prepare and serve the foods that they had eaten all week. They craned their heads through the door but the kitchen wasn't visible. The dining area was gorgeous, linens still adorning the tables, flowers scattered throughout. It would have been a treat to have eaten their meals in such a place!

Next came the bakery, still filling the hallway with the distinct smell of bread, croissants, and other French pastries that had been made fresh each day. It was a welcome relief from the scent of polishing cream that wafted around Guy and Ernesto. The bakery was large and spotless, but all activity had ceased for the moment.

Just beyond the bakery, a majestic stairway led up to the first-class section of the ship and the promenade deck. It encircled a seating area around a magnificent bar and lounge area, where Guy imagined the upper crust of society spent their evenings drinking and being entertained. The lavish style of the adornments to the stairway and sitting areas reminded him of pictures he had seen of some of the newest and most elegant hotels in Paris. Guy and Ernesto carefully polished and shined all the brass railings that lined the staircase.

The contrast between the luxury they were seeing and the poverty from which they had come contributed to their feelings of disbelief and amazement. Is this the way all Americans lived?

The *Paris* differed from the earlier French ships, which were heavily influenced by a more formal gold-accented, traditional style, by introducing a new trend called Art Nouveau in the design of the ship. This décor added a more contemporary look to the French maritime fleet.

Work on the *Paris* was begun in 1913. It was then halted in 1914 due to the hostilities surrounding World War I and resumed again in

The Grand Staircase

1919 after the war ended. Two years later, on June 5, 1921, when work on the *Paris* was completed, it was hailed as the largest vessel ever built in France. With touches of the even more avant-garde style called Art Deco, the *Paris* was the most luxurious ship on the high seas at that time.

As they continued to work, they passed more sleeping quarters and came upon another large dining room in the center of the ship. They saw tables decorated with white linens, ornate silverware, fine China settings, and cut flowers as centerpieces. The chairs boasted decorative wood backings and soft cushion seats. Guy thought the real palm trees scattered throughout the room added a warm, tropical feel. It was the lower level of the first-class dining salon on Deck C. Along with the other French liners, the *Paris* had become known for its superb food, even in second class. After experiencing such outstanding cuisine, Guy could only imagine what the food was like in first class!

This exquisite room was connected by a fancy stairway leading to the Balcony Dining Salon above. A large glass dome, supported by square pillars, was the central point of the dining area. Mirrors on the stairway reflected the light and colors of the room, which held well over one hundred tables, seating four each.

Second Class Dining Room

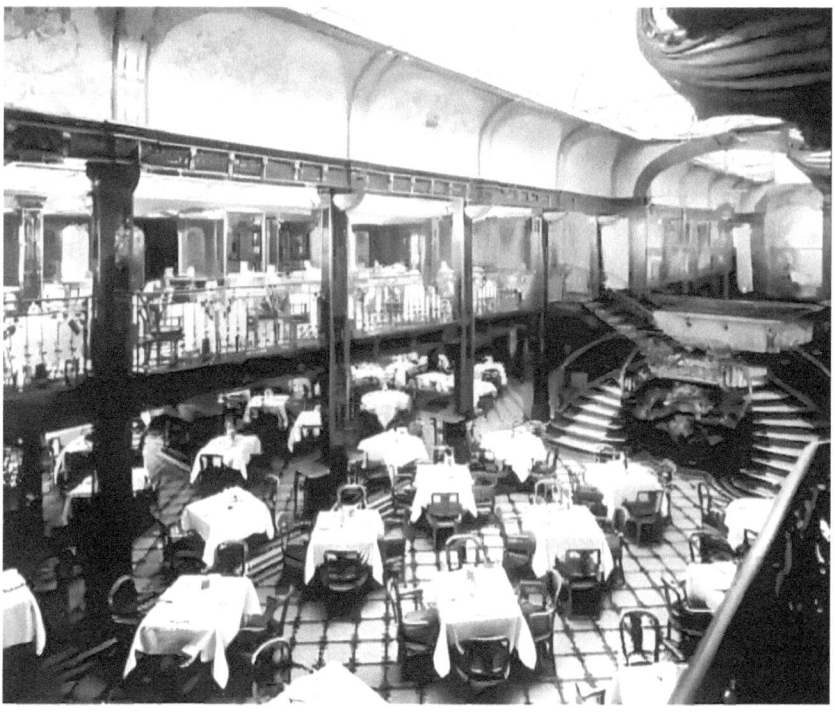

First Class Dining Salon

The friends made their way farther down the hallway and came to more cabins. These were the first-class births. Some of the rooms were luxurious suites with adjoining sitting areas and beds in a separate room. Others were just stand-alone bedrooms with a smaller lounge area in the same room. Either way, the rooms were spacious, beautifully outfitted with the latest styles of furniture and bedding. They were the ultimate in cruise comfort and convenience, some even offering a telephone to be able to call a personal butler for room service, laundry, or other needs.

First Class Stateroom

Guy and Ernesto knew nothing about the troubled history of the ship or what was about to happen to it after this smooth, uneventful voyage.

Just two years prior, the *Paris* had been involved in a tragic accident in New York Harbor. On October 16, 1927, a Norwegian cargo steamship, the SS *Besseggen*, built in 1916, was rammed by the departing SS *Paris*. The cargo ship had been anchored about half a mile south of the Statue of Liberty. According to the news reports, the *Besseggen* sunk to the bottom in less than thirty minutes. Six of the thirty-three crewmembers on the *Besseggen,* many of whom were asleep, drowned. Most of the others were rescued by several of the Staten Island Ferry boats. Blame for the accident was placed on the officers of the *Paris.* They returned back to the pier, where minor repairs were made before they continued on their way to France.

While the crew members responsible for the accident were likely disciplined, the ship continued to operate without incident between

France and New York for several more years. But that was all about to change.

Following their stowaway voyage, the ship made a successful crossing back to France and arrived back in New York on April 3. But as it was making its departure for France on April 7, the *Paris* ran aground on the Brooklyn shore in lower New York Bay. The ship's pilot had misjudged the correct waterway in thick fog. Fortunately, the ship was refloated thirty-six hours later and was able to continue the journey a few days later.

That would not be the end of the ship's troubles in 1929. Just eleven days later, on April 18, it ran aground once more off the Eddystone Lighthouse at Cornwall, a hazardous part of the English Channel. Again, the ship was refloated, but this time it took only two hours.

Whatever problems the two men were about to encounter once they managed to get off the *Paris* in America, the vessel's difficulties in 1929 would continue. The damage sustained in the grounding incidents in New York and Cornwall were minor compared to that caused by the fire that broke out on board the ship at Le Havre four months later. It began in the ship's third-class section and quickly spread to second and first class. Passenger areas were completely inundated not only by smoke but also by huge amounts of water used to put out the fire. While it was initially thought the ship would have to be scrapped after only eight years of service, it was taken to Saint-Nazaire, where it would undergo repairs and restoration for five months. Much of the damaged Art Nouveau décor was removed and replaced by even more modern Art Deco. The *Paris* survived and became more popular than ever.

But ten years later, another raging fire would eventually doom the ship.

On April 18, 1939, at ten p.m., the ship's bakery started to burn while at the dock at Le Havre. The fire spread rapidly. At the time, the *Paris* was preparing to cruise to New York with irreplaceable pieces of art to be displayed at the World's Fair. Fortunately, the art was saved. Five hours after the blaze started, the cabins on the promenade deck were completely consumed by fire. In an attempt to douse the flames, the fire brigade pumped excessive amounts of water on the ship. It eventually became top heavy because the ship's watertight compartments were fully closed, and the water could not penetrate its lower sections.

At 9:15 the next morning, the *Paris* listed over to its port side. Its huge stacks remained intact and trapped another ship, the newer SS *Normandie,* which had been docked next to the *Paris* during the fire. It was clear that it would be impossible to save the *Paris.* Two days later, the three funnels of the great ship were cut off to allow the *Normandie* to sail free.

SS Normandie *passes the stricken SS* Paris *in Le Havre harbor in April 1939.*

Of course, Guy and Ernesto were only worried about their own fate. This voyage on the SS *Paris,* their ride to America and to a new life, had concluded safely. Their lone concern now was for the next few hours. How were they going to get off the ship without detection and what would happen to them if and when they did?

Guy wondered whether his cousin Frank was already waiting for him.

CHAPTER 12

Eventually things quieted down on the ship. Guy and Ernesto weren't seeing any more customs and immigration officials snooping around, and there was little activity in the halls or cabins. It appeared to Guy that the inspection of the ship had been completed. All the passengers had disembarked. The only people left were the ship's workers, cleaning the hallways and rooms as he and Ernesto were attempting to do as conscientiously as the others. Every so often, one of the other crew members would look at them with an inquisitive glance, obviously wondering why they had never seen these two before. But since there were over six hundred crew members aboard the *Paris,* not everyone would be a familiar face. No suspicions were raised, and nothing was ever said.

Guy and Ernesto had survived another part of their harrowing ordeal without detection. At least for now. They both sensed a feeling of relief, but with it came a heightened feeling of anticipation. So many questions remained for Guy—how would he get off the ship, would Frank be waiting, where would he go from here?

There was still so much they didn't know.

After a few more hours, the two crew members responsible for them approached as they worked and told them it was all clear. The inspectors had left the ship. The *Paris* would stay docked in New York for another three days. Tomorrow they would have to get off the ship. They still didn't explain how that was to occur. He could tell from their demeanor that the less he knew in advance, the better, so he didn't ask any questions. It was already late in the day, and the crew members informed them there would be nothing served in the dining room that night so they wouldn't be getting a meal in their cabin as usual. They told Guy and Ernesto they would take them to the second-class kitchen and would have something there for them to eat.

The crew members accompanied Guy and Ernesto back to their cabin, that section of the ship that had not yet been cleaned. They changed from their work overalls into the casual clothes they had been given in Paris and were escorted to the second-class kitchen. They were the only ones there.

Guy and Ernesto asked where everyone else was. The two crew members explained that all the other workers on the crew had their own cabins in the lower part of the ship, their own dining facility, and dinner was being prepared there for them that night. Some would have already left the ship for a night out in New York City. Many others would have the day off tomorrow and would leave the ship in the morning.

Guy and Ernesto enjoyed a dinner of sandwiches, cheese, fruit, and a nice French wine. Both were hungry and tired from working all day, something they had not done since leaving Paris six days before. The day outside their cabin, as intense as it had been, was a memorable one for Guy. He had enjoyed seeing some of this remarkable ship. Now this meal—the simplest he had eaten all week—was more like what he was used to back in Paris. He savored all of it. He assumed this would be his last aboard the ship, and he had no idea where his next one would be.

When they had finished eating, they were escorted back to their cabin and told not to go anywhere. There was still a chance that someone could be suspicious if they were seen leaving or entering this cabin in second class. All the paying passengers had left the ship by now, so it would be unusual to see people in this part of the ship, especially in one of the cabins. The crew members said they would return in the morning to get them off the ship.

How that was to occur was still a mystery.

Ernesto was less sure of what was to happen to him. His brother in Detroit could not have received word that he was coming yet. It had been less than a week since he had asked Michel if he could go along with Guy—certainly not enough time for the letter he had hurriedly sent to get there.

Would the third time be a charm for him? Ernesto knew if he didn't make it this time, he might not have enough courage and will-power to try again.

After a restless night spent anticipating what would happen the next day, Guy awoke to a knock on the cabin door early the next morning. The time had come. They would now attempt to enter the United States. The crew members collected their work clothes and cleaned up any trace that there had been someone unauthorized in the cabin. Guy and Ernesto were in the casual clothing they had been given in Paris and packed their wrinkled suits into the suitcase they had been given on the ship. They would exit the ship as crew members going out for the day in New York.

They handed Guy and Ernesto each a day pass and told them if anybody asks, Guy was to say his name was Michel, the name on his pass. He thought this was odd, since it was the name of the stranger that had brought them from Paris to the ship in Le Havre. Was this a code or merely a coincidence? How could anyone else know about Michel? Once again, Guy didn't ask any questions. Ernesto was to say his name was Pierre. Since they both spoke French fluently, if they were asked any other questions, they were simply to say they were crew members on leave for the day. One of the men picked up the suit-case. "Follow us."

They walked out separately from the cabin. Guy went with the kitchen manager. Ernesto followed with the cook. Guy wondered why they were being escorted individually instead of together as they had been when they got on the boat.

He also wondered if the crew members might be anticipating a coordinated attempt by Guy and Ernesto to escape from them once they were off the ship. This would be more difficult separately. *Why would we want to escape? Escape what?* Or maybe it was to increase the chances that one would make it off the ship if the other was de-tained and questioned.

That must be it. That made more sense.

As they approached the exit leading to the ramp for crew members, they noticed two uniformed guards at the door. Guy and Ernesto acted as if they expected to be questioned—they each had a pass—and greeted the guards as they got closer. They casually made small talk with the friends they were accompanying on their day off together in New York. Guy and the kitchen manager talked about their shared love of fishing. Following close behind, Ernesto and the cook appeared to be discussing their plans to explore the city. Other crew members on passes had been leaving the ship through this exit all morning, and the two guards barely paid attention as the four of them walked leisurely by and off the ship.

As they made their way down the ramp, Guy noticed two men standing at the entrance of the ramp, looking up at them. The men, dressed in suits, appeared to be expecting them. He did not see Frank anywhere. Were these men officials who were onto them and about to make an arrest? Or were they part of the illegal operation and involved in the stowaway? Guy couldn't be sure as the men continued to watch them come down the ramp.

They stepped onto American soil. Guy could not believe he had made it this far and was now off the boat and in the United States. He had to consciously control the emotions he was feeling, since he still had no idea who these two men were. As he looked around, what he saw astounded him. Buildings taller than anything he had ever seen rose toward the sky in all directions. Noise, congestion, and traffic was everywhere. Shops, businesses, and restaurants lined the street they were on. New York City was already alive, and the day had just begun. What would it be like at night? He imagined how magnificent it must be with lights in the buildings, people out walking and taking in the sights and smells of this great city. He realized then he had come so far from his little village in Italy, and even from the more subdued, historic architecture of Paris. This was unlike anything he had seen before.

Luxury Liner SS Normandie *(Paris's sister ship) sits off piers in NYC in 1935*

His feelings of amazement and wonder were cut short by the reality of what was happening to him next. They walked together across the street toward a small restaurant opposite the docks. The two men waiting for them followed but said nothing to them or to the crew members. Guy and Ernesto entered the restaurant with the crew members and were led to a table.

"Sit here, but don't act suspiciously," they were told. There was no one else in the dark room except two other men already seated at a table on the opposite side. It was far enough away in the dim light that Guy could not make out any of their features.

The men who had been waiting for them at the bottom of the ramp did not follow them in. Guy thought that was strange, but since they hadn't been arrested, he now assumed those men were there to ensure the crew members delivered Guy and Ernesto to the right place. Certainly, they were getting paid for this, so someone had to confirm the job was completed before any money was handed over.

Frank was not in the restaurant as Guy had hoped. *Strange*, he thought.

The crew members walked over to the table across the room where the two other men were seated. A waiter came to the table and offered Guy and Ernesto some coffee. He poured them both a cup. Guy watched intently as the crew members spoke to the other men, but he could not hear what they were saying. After a lengthy conversation, he saw one of the crew members hand the two men a letter. Guy assumed it was the same letter the officers had received from Michel when Guy and Ernesto were getting on the ship in Le Havre. It was probably a contract of some kind, stipulating the terms of payment that had been agreed upon to get Guy over to the United States secretly and illegally as a *clandestino*—a stowaway.

As they continued talking, the men at the table carefully studied the letter. Guy saw them signal to each other and to the crew members that it appeared all was in order. The two men then gazed at Ernesto. They must have been discussing his situation and how they would handle that. As far as Guy knew, no one had yet paid to get Ernesto here. Had they already let his brother in Detroit know he was in New York? He assumed Ernesto was also concerned about it, but now that they were off the ship, he hadn't shown any worry. He expected his brother would take care of it as soon as he was contacted.

The crew members stood up and walked toward Guy and Ernesto.

"We're leaving you now with these two. We wish you good luck here in the United States."

Just like that. They were being left with another group of strangers. Before Guy even had a chance to digest this new piece of information, they exchanged good-byes, and the crew members turned and walked out of the restaurant.

The other two men had followed the crew members to the table and were now alone with Guy and Ernesto. Finally, Guy was able to get a good look at them. From their looks and manner of dress, they appeared to be Italian.

Guy spoke first. If his instinct was correct, they would understand.

"Where's my cousin? I was told by the guy who came to my house in France that he'd be here waiting for me when I got off the ship. I was assured I would meet him here."

One of the men then sternly rebuked Guy in Italian. Now there was no doubt.

"Stop talking!" he demanded. "You have no idea of the kind of bad trouble you're in. You had better keep your mouth shut!"

At that moment, Guy felt a lump in his throat, a tightness in his chest, and the fear that he had been denying all along resurfaced. He realized that it may all have been a fraud. Had he been lied to? How could he have let himself fall into this trap? He was now alone in America in the hands of these criminals. Just when he thought the nightmare was over, it seemed as if it was just beginning.

As difficult as it was, Guy accepted the likelihood of a terrifying possibility—*his cousin knew nothing about this.*

Frank would not be waiting for him.

CHAPTER 13

Disbelief, anger, and fear gripped Guy as he thought about what he had just heard. What did this belligerent stranger mean by "the bad trouble he was in?" What kind of trouble? Had Frank done something to upset these men? Maybe Frank had exposed the stowaway scheme to the authorities. Guy quickly dismissed that idea because he believed Frank would not have done anything to put him in danger. More likely, his cousin had no clue that Guy was here in the United States. It was the only possibility that made sense.

Guy thought about the severity of his situation—illegally in America, no identification, no American money, not able to speak a word of English, and in the hands of what appeared to be mobsters. What could be worse for him? Other than Ernesto—who was now figuratively in the same boat—or his friend and former landlord back in Paris, no one else even knew where he was. The letters he had written on the ship were still in his pocket. How or when would he even be able to get them mailed? While he desperately tried to think of ways out of this mess, he realized there was only one. He hadn't considered it before because he had not seen this coming. The sight of those two suspicious men waiting for them at the bottom of the ramp flashed again in his mind.

Now he wished he and Ernesto had discussed how they would escape. He sadly accepted the realization that—even if they had discussed it—the chances of a successful escape were slim.

They had been captured. Ironically, not in the way he had dreaded all along.

The two men led Guy and Ernesto toward the exit. The older one, who had angrily reprimanded Guy when he started asking questions, was short, overweight, and had a foul expression and demeanor. It appeared the scar on his face was from a knife wound that had healed badly. He looked frightening to Guy—someone not to mess with.

The younger of the two was thin and good-looking and could have been the son or nephew of the older man. His facial expression showed a kinder, sympathetic attitude toward Guy and Ernesto, as if he clearly understood how frightened they must be. The younger man spoke Italian with the older one, who told him to keep an eye on them while he went outside to get a cab. The young man carried a suitcase—the one that Guy and Ernesto had been given on the ship with the suits they had worn from Paris. Somehow the crew members from the ship had delivered it to the two men in the restaurant. Guy had not seen it before now.

Only after the taxi had shown up were they led outside and shoved into the back of a spacious black automobile.

March 13, 1929, was a warm spring day in New York, much like it had been in Paris only seven days before. Temperatures were in the mid-sixties with a few clouds, suggesting a chance of showers, but they knew it would not matter to them if it did rain.

They would not be going for a stroll in New York City.

It was difficult to see anything from the back seat of the taxi. Massive steel and concrete buildings created huge walls on both sides of the street, blocking any light until they reached a cross street, and the sky would temporarily appear again. He felt as if he were in a canyon. Cars, bicycles, buses, and street cars crowded each block as they made their way into the heart of the city. They passed men pushing carts loaded with fruits, vegetables, and boxes of all shapes and sizes. People all over were in a rush to get somewhere, yet the traffic moved slowly.

Traffic on Fifth Avenue in New York City in 1929

At each block, the taxi would have to slow or stop to await a signal to cross. Tall bronze poles, some with a statue of a helmeted Greek god on the top, dotted each corner and signaled either red or green to direct the flow of traffic through the city. Although Paris had recently begun the use of lighted signals to manage traffic, there were few in use in the 1920s. At the busy intersections in Paris, police officers were still widely used to direct traffic. Guy was fascinated by the unusual sights he was able to see with his limited view of this new world.

The taxi ride took twenty minutes. Guy had no idea in which direction they were traveling, but they had probably gone only ten to fifteen kilometers (six to nine miles) in traffic. He had seen no bridges and no water, so he assumed they were still somewhere in the city. He knew from having seen maps of New York City, that it was mostly on an island. There was a section where most of the Italian immigrants lived in a crowded ghetto, tenement houses surrounded by Italian shops, businesses, restaurants, and outdoor markets. He expected they would be going there, but he didn't see any of that.

Instead, they came to a stop outside a nice-looking three-story house. As they were led inside, Guy could see it was a quiet neighborhood, certainly not the ghetto he was expecting. The houses were spaced close to each other but seemed respectable, well-built, and maintained. Whoever owned these places must have money, he thought.

They climbed a set of stairs to a second-floor apartment and were greeted by a woman who was cooking something that smelled delightful. She was middle-aged, perhaps the wife or sister of the older man, maybe the mother of the younger one. As she continued to prepare lunch for them, she spoke in Italian and made them feel welcome in her house. Guy could tell she was nice, not like the older man he had encountered. It was obvious she wanted company and enjoyed her new guests. She talked to them as if they were good friends and never mentioned anything about how they had arrived, their current situation, or what was going to happen to them.

She served them a wonderful lunch of Italian macaroni, meatballs, and wine. Guy was impressed with her cooking. It reminded him of how his mother had cooked when he was a young boy living at home—nothing fancy, just delicious and sweet-smelling peasant food.

The two men, talking in another room, suddenly appeared and interrupted the conversation with the woman. They sat at the table and ate lunch with Guy and Ernesto. Nothing was said. The woman did not sit with them or eat. She busied herself with washing pots and pans and did not look at them. Her demeanor had changed from a pleasant, friendly one to a more subdued and subservient, almost invisible, presence.

When lunch was over, the older man finally spoke.

"You two stay here now, in that room. Do not look out of the windows or even go near them. Just stay in the parlor, read the newspaper, smoke cigarettes, but don't go near the windows!"

Guy wondered whether that warning was meant to keep him and Ernesto from discovering where they were. It could have also been a precaution to keep outsiders from seeing strange faces in the windows. Either way, they would take no chances. It did not look good.

Then the older man said, "Now you're going to write a letter to your cousin to let him know you're here in New York."

That finally confirmed what Guy had been thinking since he got off the ship. Frank knew nothing about this. The "bad trouble he was in" was becoming clear.

What was Frank able to do? He lived near Boston, not New York. It would take at least a week for a letter to get to him. What was to happen in the meantime?

It was to be a short letter. Guy was told what to write:

"I'm here in New York. You must come to rescue me with $600. I hope you come.

Your cousin, Gaetano DeSantis."

Guy knew that $600 was a huge amount of money for his cousin. He doubted whether Frank would even be able to earn that much in a year as a baker. How was he ever going to be able to come up with that kind of money? The grim reality of his situation was now perfectly clear.

He was being held for ransom in an extortion scheme.

CHAPTER 14

That evening, "Scarface"—as Guy thought of him—mailed the letter to Frank's home from a nearby post office. At the same time, a telegram was sent to Frank at the bakery where he worked in Newton, Massachusetts. Guy wondered how these men had all that information about his cousin, including the address of his place of employment. How had they obtained it? Guy hoped that the telegram would arrive quickly, but since it was already late in the day on Wednesday, March 13, the telegram would not be delivered until the next day. Ernesto was told to write a similar letter to his brother in Detroit and a telegram was also sent.

Now all they could do was wait.

Beds had been set up for them in a room down a narrow hallway from the parlor. Sal, the younger man, also slept in the same room. He was not going to take his eyes off Guy and Ernesto and was with them constantly, day and night. Guy noticed something that terrified him—Sal was carrying a pistol in the waistband of his pants.

There would be no chance of escape.

During the day, the woman was always there, cleaning the house and making coffee and all their meals. She remained quiet except when neither of her two acquaintances were close enough to hear her. She told them her name was Carmella and would make small talk. Yet she never spoke of the situation facing Guy and Ernesto. It was clear that she feared the two men who shared her house and was afraid for Guy and Ernesto as well.

When they were alone for a few minutes, Carmella revealed to Guy and Ernesto that she was the older man's sister. His name was Pauli. Sal was her son.

In the parlor, there were several books in Italian. Guy tried to read one of them, but it was about the mob and men killing each other, so he quickly put it down. He didn't need to read about crime and gangsters. He was living it.

The newspapers were also in Italian—*Il Progresso Italo-Americano*—one of the first daily newspapers in the United States. Guy found it interesting, but it mainly covered American news. He was hoping to get news about what was happening in Italy.

In one of the articles from that day's edition, there appeared to be some kind of uprising at the southern border of the United States. It involved rebels from the country of Mexico led by a man named General Escobar. Some were concerned that a possible conflict between the United States and Mexico would result. The cause of the rebellion was difficult for Guy to understand, but it was viewed as a matter fraught with danger to US-Mexico relations.

Guy knew from the limited amount of history he had studied that religious wars were a common occurrence in Europe. *Would it happen here too? New York is far from Mexico, but would it be safe?*

Another news story in the paper from the previous day caught his eye. Eleven steamships were to arrive in New York from foreign ports on March 12. It even cited his very own SS *Paris*, arriving from Le Havre. It mentioned the names of some of the more prominent passengers onboard. On the *Paris*, it named two passengers who must have been in first class—Lady Hunt and Lady Gordon. Who were they? Perhaps they were from British royalty. They certainly weren't names you would hear in Southern Italy. The article said that a total of 4,506 passengers were expected on the eleven ships. He knew for sure that was at least two short in the count, maybe more with the potential number of stowaways that ten other ships would bring in.

In addition to the *France* and the *Paris*, the list of ships arriving on March 12 included the *Muenchen* from Bremen, the *Antonia* and *Albertic* both from Liverpool, *Ebro* from Valparaiso (Chile), *Tivives* from Barrios (Guatemala), *Avon* from Bermuda, *Orizaba* from Havana, *Duchess* from the West Indies, and *Mongolia* from San Francisco. It must have been a busy day at Ellis Island. Although the number of passengers being processed every day had declined considerably over the last four years, the facility averaged 5,000 people a day.

That was one problem that he and Ernesto had not faced. However, looking back over the last twelve hours, he gladly would have endured the three to five hours the inspection would have taken. It would have been much easier than suffering through what could be days of fear and worry. How long would it take for his cousin to get here? Would Frank be able to come up with the money? What if he could not—what would they do with Guy then?

As much as he tried to concentrate on other things, these thoughts and doubts constantly plagued him as he tried to pass the time in his new captivity.

So he kept reading. Thankfully, there were a few articles about the political power structure in Italy. *Il Progresso* was clearly favorable to Mussolini after he gained power and declared himself dictator in 1925. What Guy had read in the French press about Mussolini's accomplishments did not convince him that it was a good thing. He disagreed with fascism, racism, class warfare, and almost everything else Mussolini stood for, except maybe getting the trains to run on time. He particularly disliked the violence of Mussolini's paramilitary groups that targeted labor unions. But he could not foresee the amount of damage this man would inflict on Italy and the rest of the world in the next decade.

He glanced up at Sal who sat on a couch across the room. The pistol protruded from his waistband. Guy delved back into the paper like it was salvation.

There were other articles about raising money to erect statues in New York for Italian heroes like Garibaldi, Verdi, Verrazzano, and Dante. There were stories that campaigned for Italians who were considered the victims of injustice. It was obvious that powerful Italian Americans ran the newspaper—*the prominenti*—who sought to integrate Italian Americans into the fabric of American society. *How will we ever integrate into the fabric of American society?* Guy wondered.

He thought about his family and friends back in Italy. The last letter he had received from a half-brother in Italy, who could read and write, spoke of a continuation of *la miseria* that he had left behind six years prior when he went to France. As poor as he knew it to be, he now longed for the peace and beauty of his ancestral home. He yearned for the companionship and comfort of his friends and family back in Italy.

At the same time Guy was reading the newspaper on Wednesday, March 13, Frank's boss in Newton received the telegram delivered to his bakery.

"Frank! Telegram!" Frank's face fell. Bad news from his family in Italy, he suspected. Why else would someone send a telegram? He had never received one before.

He carefully opened the envelope and read something totally unexpected.

WE HAVE YOUR COUSIN GAETANO HERE IN NY STOP IF YOU WANT TO SEE HIM ALIVE AGAIN SHOW UP ALONE WITH $600 TO THIS ADDRESS . . .

Frank was in shock and disbelief. He read it again and then to his boss.

He said, "I don't know anything about my cousin coming to America. Something looks suspicious about this."

He remembered writing to his cousin about joining him in the United States. At that time, Guy said he would like to come but would have to earn more money in Paris before he could even think about it. Then the immigration laws changed, and the door to America had been closed to him. The last time they had written to each other was about six months earlier, but there was no mention about Guy coming to New York. How could Guy have arranged this without him knowing? It was obvious to Frank that if he were really here, he must have come illegally as a stowaway.

But what if this telegram itself was a hoax? What if he were not even here? This could be *la mano nera*—the Black Hand—trying to extort money from Frank as they had been doing to people and businesses for a decade, especially in New York.

Even if it were true, and Guy really was in New York, how was Frank ever going to raise $600? He didn't have that kind of money in the bank. He could not even earn that much in a year. There was no time to verify any of this with his cousin in Paris. If he tried to send Guy a telegram, that would take days. And if Guy weren't in Paris to accept a telegram, who would be able to respond to it? Would he even get a reply? Did anyone in Italy know where he was? What could he do?

Frank realized he had no choice but to take the threat seriously and would have to plan a way to quickly raise the money.

He needed to get to New York as soon as possible to rescue his cousin.

CHAPTER 15

Frank faced two problems simultaneously. If it were true that Guy was in the United States, he did not want his cousin in danger any longer than necessary. Time was of the essence. All he knew from the telegram was the address in New York City where he was to meet these men. He had no name or way to contact them. He would have to go to New York to find out whether his cousin was really here or if this was simply a fraud—or some kind of extortion scheme.

The first problem was coming up with the $600. How long would that take? He had some ideas but was not sure he would be able to get the entire amount. He had enough in the bank to personally fund some of it, but he would still be at least $500 short. The men Frank knew were mostly immigrants with jobs that didn't pay much more than $500 in annual wages. It would be a difficult task. What would they do to Guy if Frank could not raise enough? The thought terrified him. He just had to find a way.

Then, once he had the money, he would have to get to New York City. A train or bus would not get him where he needed to go, and his car would not be dependable on that long a drive. It would take at least five hours to drive from his home in Newton to New York, assuming there were no breakdowns or accidents along the way. No, driving that far was not an option. He would just have to get as close as possible by train, then take a taxi to the meeting point.

He thought about the time it would take. The telegram was dated

Wednesday, March 13. It was now Thursday morning. If it took him another two days to get the money and get to New York, he would arrive there by Saturday. If Guy was there, he would have already spent at least three days in captivity. Hopefully, Frank could get him out that day. That's if everything went smoothly.

Frank spent the rest of the day visiting his *paisanos* in the Newton area. Some even knew Guy personally, since they had come from the same small town in Italy. He showed them the telegram and explained to them what he knew, which wasn't more than what was on the telegram. He shared his concern that this might be a setup, but he had no choice but to take it seriously. Frank still hadn't received the letter that had been mailed to his house from New York, in Guy's handwriting, and with his signature.

He called people he knew in Mamaroneck, New York, an affluent suburb about twenty-five miles north of New York City. A large community of Italians lived there, and the town and surrounding area were growing rapidly, creating jobs and opportunities for these recent immigrants. In the early 1920s, it had been known as a center of moviemaking on the East Coast.

Frank and Guy had friends from their hometown of Arce, Italy, living there. These *Arcese* encouraged Frank to come, and they would gather whatever funds they could raise and provide Frank a place to stay. By the end of the day on Thursday, Frank had received enough loans from his friends in Newton and commitments from the Italians in Mamaroneck, that he was hopeful he would have the $600 he needed.

On Friday, Frank took the train from Boston to New York and was met at the station in Mamaroneck. He was warmly greeted by his friends, who were happy to see him but concerned about what might be happening to Guy. They discussed the situation over dinner, made sure they had gathered enough money, and came up with a plan.

Frank was to go to New York City, to the address shown on the telegram, early on Saturday morning, and determine if Guy was actually there. His plan was to leave the ransom money in Mamaroneck as a precaution. Once he determined that his cousin was being held—and could physically see him—he would go back to Mamaroneck to get it, return to the city, and make the swap for Guy. A lot of people had entrusted their bank savings and whatever cash they had under the mattress to help Frank raise the $600 to rescue Guy.

He was not going to risk losing it on some foolish and fruitless escapade.

Carlo, a well-respected labor union delegate in Mamaroneck, offered to accompany Frank to the address for the meeting. He looked at the telegram and where they would have to go.

He said, "Frank, I'll take you in my automobile. It won't take long."

Even though the telegram warned Frank to come alone, the thought of what he would find unnerved him, and he welcomed Carlo's offer. He was not at all familiar with the city and would not know his way around if things went badly. It would be good to have a friend with a car if they needed to make a quick escape.

The drive to the address took less than an hour. It was actually a small storefront in an Italian neighborhood. Carlo found a parking spot on the opposite side of the street, about a block away. Frank crossed the street and walked to the address he had been given. Carlo stayed in the car, keeping a careful watch on Frank as he walked into the store.

There was an old man behind the counter inside the store, a small grocery market.

"I'm looking for this address," Frank said as he approached the counter.

The man looked at the telegram, read the address, and said to Frank, "You have the right place. This is the correct address. But I don't know who Gaetano is or anything about what you're looking for. I'm sorry, but I can't help you."

Crushed and confused, Frank thanked him and left the store. He started across the street to tell Carlo the grim news when he heard another man calling to him from the vicinity of the store he had just left.

"Wait, who are you looking for?" the stranger shouted.

Frank was momentarily startled and did not see where this man had come from. He had seen no one else in the store. Was he hiding inside the store or somewhere close by? Maybe the address he had been given was not really where he was to meet after all. Maybe it was just a way for him to be observed—to make sure Frank had not alerted the police and brought them as well.

Frank turned to face the man and said, "I'm looking for this address. I'm supposed to meet a guy here."

A short, heavy man with an ugly scar on his face walked toward him. He appeared dangerous, and not knowing who he was, Frank was unwilling to say too much.

"I'm the fellow you're looking for," the man said. "You can call me Pauli. Do you have the money?"

Frank hadn't mentioned anything about money, so he assumed Pauli was the man he was supposed to meet. How else would he know about the money? He looked at Frank suspiciously and nervously glanced around the area to make sure there was no one else watching them. He didn't see Carlo parked a block away, waiting for Frank.

Frank replied, "Yes, I have the money, but I didn't bring it. Before I'm going to pay you this kind of money, I want to see my cousin. If he is really here, I want to see him and talk to him."

"You can't! Your cousin is still on the boat," the man said angrily. He did not expect this uneducated Italian to think about possibilities such as this.

"Well, he may still be on the boat," Frank replied, holding in his nerves, "but if he is, I want to see him. You need to get him off the boat first."

Realizing Frank had cleverly thought out this well-planned response—and that he was not going to be convinced without seeing Guy—Pauli paused and thought for a few seconds.

"Okay, your cousin is out," Pauli admitted. "He's already off the boat and in a house somewhere in the city. He's safe. If you want to see him, come with me."

He started to walk away from Frank and down the street.

"Do you have a car to take me?" Frank asked.

"No, we'll have to take a street car. The people holding your cousin do not have an automobile, and neither do I."

"I have a friend parked over there. He's my *paisano* and has an automobile. He'll drive us," Frank replied, while pointing in the direction of Carlo's car.

Pauli suddenly stopped walking and looked angrily into Frank's face, realizing that Frank had not come alone.

"Who is the most important person to this Gaetano DeSantis? Is it you or your friend in the car?"

"It's me, of course. I'm his cousin," said Frank.

"Then *you* have to come with me—*alone*. Not the other guy."

Frank reluctantly nodded, walked over to where Carlo was parked, and explained what was happening. Carlo had been watching the two men from a distance. He could see they were talking but could not hear the conversation. When Frank told him that he would have to go alone with this man to supposedly see his cousin, Carlo looked deeply concerned. How would he know where they had gone? What would he do if Frank didn't come back? How long would he wait?

Carlo did not think leaving his friend alone with this stranger was a good idea at all. Was Frank even sure this proposed arrangement was legitimate, and that he was not going to be harmed or held hostage as well?

No, he wasn't sure.

But it was a chance Frank had to take.

CHAPTER 16

Carlo watched apprehensively as his friend walked off with this stranger—a mobster. He kept thinking the worst. Would he see Frank again today? Where would he even begin to look for him if he didn't? He accepted the fact that he would now just have to wait and hope Frank knew what he was doing.

Frank's concern for his cousin overcame his anxiety as he followed the gangster to the nearest trolley station a few blocks away. After a short ride on the streetcar, he was told to get off and get into a taxi. Pauli was obviously making it difficult for them to be followed. After a few miles, the taxi let them off at an apartment building located in a quiet neighborhood surrounded by other two- or three-story apartment buildings, not a tenement as he had anticipated. There was no one around except for a few people walking nearby but paying no attention to them. Would Guy be here?

Frank was led into the first floor of a house with a room that had no furniture except for a large round table. There was no one inside the house.

"Now you wait here," Pauli said. "Don't be scared. Just pretend this is your house, and don't be afraid of anybody."

Frank watched Pauli leave the house, hopefully, to get Guy and bring him here. After a few long minutes, the door opened, and another man walked into the house, approached the table, and said to Frank angrily, "Who are you?"

He wore a long beard, probably to compensate for his thinning hair, and appeared to Frank to be mad at someone or something. Frank remembered being told to not be afraid of anybody, but this guy was so agitated that Frank couldn't help being shocked by his behavior.

"Somebody brought me here, and I was told to wait," Frank replied.

"Are you Frank DeSantis?"

"Yes."

BOOM! The man slammed the door and left. What was that all about? The only thing Frank could think of was whether this man was angry with Pauli. Maybe this guy had not known of Frank's insistence on seeing his cousin first before any money was exchanged. Perhaps this man did not agree with him being taken here, possibly exposing them or their location. This hadn't been part of their plan.

Would this argument endanger Guy or even him? Frank wondered.

Maybe he should just get out now while he could. The door hadn't been locked, so Frank knew he could get out. But would it be a wise move? No, he wanted to see his cousin—he would stay and wait.

Meanwhile, Pauli was on his way to get Guy.

Back at the house, Sal kept watch on Guy and Ernesto, making sure they were clearly able to see the pistol now protruding from his back pocket.

Pauli—Scarface, as Guy called him—came into the house, and after a brief discussion with Sal that Guy could not hear, said, "You're coming with me. Your cousin is here and wants to see you."

Guy was elated by the prospect of finally seeing Frank but tried not to show his excitement. He had been disappointed so many times before on this journey, and he did not want to set himself up for another one. But he couldn't help thinking that this time would be different. Would he finally be released and able to go home with his cousin as a free man?

He smiled at Ernesto, and they exchanged hugs and the customary kisses on the cheek.

"If you don't come back," Ernesto said, "good luck, my friend. After what we've been through together, I hope this turns out well for you."

"Thank you for wanting to come and for your company. It would have been so much more difficult alone," Guy said. He embraced Ernesto one more time, tears starting to form at the thought of what might happen to either of them. He wondered whether he would ever see Ernesto again.

Ernesto gave Guy his brother's address in Detroit and asked him to write. Hopefully, he would be there soon. His brother had been contacted, was told to come to New York with the money, and the gangsters were awaiting a response from him.

Guy followed Pauli down the street and onto a trolley that had just stopped.

He couldn't read English and had no idea what the signs said. He boarded like everyone else and tried to look inconspicuous. Pauli kept looking at him, anticipating that Guy would try to run. Guy guessed that he probably had a gun hidden under his jacket. He wasn't going to take any chances. He was too close now.

After a long ride, they arrived at the house where Frank was supposedly waiting. Guy's apprehension grew as he realized that if this were true, he would be seeing his cousin for the first time in eight years. He remembered saying good-bye to Frank as he left Italy for America in 1921, and he had no idea when he would see Frank again. Guy certainly hadn't imagined it would be under these circumstances.

"We get off at the next stop," Pauli said.

He followed Pauli on foot for a few blocks to an apartment house. As they approached, Guy noticed nothing unusual about it and no one was waiting outside. The neighborhood was quiet and looked like it would be a nice place to live. The house had two levels, with an outdoor porch on the first level, and stairs inside leading to the second floor, which had its own enclosed balcony above the front porch.

They walked through the front porch and entered the house without knocking. Then he saw Frank, sitting alone at a large round table.

As soon as they made eye contact, it was as if they were back in Italy together, playing soccer as teenagers, with not a care in the world. The seriousness of their present situation and the danger they both were facing vanished for just a few moments. A feeling of hope returned to Guy in a way that he had not experienced since he had left France. An assurance that this would turn out well overcame him as he kissed his cousin on each cheek. For the first time, he was optimistic that the decision he had made in Paris over a week ago would turn out well, just like all the other tough decisions he had made in his life.

He didn't know how this would occur, but the feeling was strong, and he trusted it.

Frank embraced his cousin and said, "Gaetano, I'm so happy to see you and know you're all right. You're really here! I wasn't sure because I had no idea you were coming."

Frank couldn't say much because Pauli was listening intently to their conversation. While Guy thought he would now be rescued, Frank knew he would have to leave him there for at least another few hours. He could not tell him what had happened since he received the telegram, how his friends from Italy had gathered around him, or how they had helped him raise enough money for the ransom.

Guy said, "Yes, I've been treated well since arriving in New York, but I'm looking forward to getting out of this." He didn't tell Frank about the younger man with the gun who was watching them.

Frank said, "I didn't bring any money on this trip, but I have it in another town close by with my friends. I have to go back there now, but I'll come back tonight with the money. Then we can leave, and you'll come with me."

Guy felt a hollowness in his chest when he heard the money wasn't there. He clenched his teeth and tried to steel himself against the waiting. *Another opportunity for something else to go wrong,* he thought. Although he anxiously hoped his cousin had come prepared to get him out now, he accepted the fact there had to be one more step before he would be able to go free. He knew that Frank was being cautious and that they were dealing with a large amount of money. He didn't know it was other people's money. And they were dealing with men who couldn't be trusted. He was determined not to let his impatience, or any fear, deter his optimism. Just hearing Frank say those words would be enough to sustain him until tonight.

They embraced again and took each other's hand.

"We'll see you tonight, don't worry. We'll see you tonight," Frank said.

Frank was then told he could leave and how to get back to his friend Carlo who was still waiting for him.

Carlo was relieved when he saw Frank walking toward the car. The ordeal had taken several hours, but now they would head back to Mamaroneck, have dinner, get the money, and return to get Guy.

Guy was escorted out of the house, and he and Pauli retraced the route they had taken to get there by foot and trolley.

They were to meet later that night at the same place Frank had encountered Pauli earlier that day, the address on the telegram.

This time with the money.

CHAPTER 17

As they drove back to Mamaroneck, Frank and Carlo discussed their plan to return to rescue Guy from the clutches of the mob. Frank recounted the instructions he had received. They were to meet at the same address at seven p.m.—carrying the money in an envelope so it could easily be seen.

Although they could not be sure, they assumed this was a plot carried out by the Black Hand, an organized crime syndicate that had been terrorizing immigrants, mostly Italians, in New York, Chicago, New Orleans, San Francisco, and other major cities in the United States for fifty years. Frank and Carlo had read stories about the *Mano Nera*, knew about the domestic extortion threats, bombings, and kidnappings attributed to this group, but these had occurred many years prior. During the first decade of the 1900s, there had been a concerted effort from law enforcement, led by teams of resolute police officers—many of whom were of Italian American descent—to shut it down. While some of the officers died in the ensuing battles with these gangs, many arrests were made, and the ferocity of the activity had been reduced considerably. However, it was an organization that played for keeps. There would not be any negotiating with them, and Frank took the ransom demand very seriously.

They were familiar with many of the tactics employed by this ruthless organization in Italian American communities across America. Yet none of their friends had heard about this particular scheme; they hadn't known anyone else who had been caught up in it. It wasn't the work of a *padrone*—in that case payment for the trip would have already been received in advance by the immigrant or a company sponsoring him. Then regular payments would be required for the immigrant to work, have a place to live, or protect his family. And since the Immigration Act of 1924 was instated, use of a *padrone* to lure people to America had virtually disappeared. No, this was different. They were holding Guy hostage until someone paid the ransom to free him. It had to be organized crime.

As early as the turn of the century, stories had circulated about the brutality of the Black Hand Society. Even though the amount of criminal activity among Italian immigrants was no greater than that of any other ethnic group in America, or for the population in general, it was an ongoing source of embarrassment and humiliation because of the publicity it received. The majority of Italians had come to America to earn an honest living and to raise their families with opportunities they would never have in their home country. But these stories, often brutal and vicious, made headlines. The media—and even some politicians—played on the fear and hatred of these gangs, and it tainted the view of Italian Americans in general.

For instance, over twenty years earlier, in 1908, an article had appeared in the *Boston Globe* entitled "Pay or Be Killed." The article quoted several ransom letters sent to a wealthy hotel owner in Boston, who decided to disclose the letters to the police in spite of the threats. Because of his courage to risk his life—and that of his family—the suspects were subsequently caught and arrested. The letters were determined to have come from a branch of the Black Hand Society operating in the Boston area.

"Dear Friend: By sending you this letter we renew our acquaintance. If you remember you favored us when we stole your child. Our company expects help from you because we want to live and this has got to be secret, not even your family is to know anything. So if it leaks out it is going to cause you ruin and death. If you do as we request we will let you alone and let you and your family live a happy life. We are going away from America and going elsewhere, and we want $1,000. To save your life you have got to send the money or take the consequences of being "killed by SSL." Therefore think it over. If you value your life and do not want to die, send us what we ask. I will also state that a company of nine of us visited your hotel Feb 9 and inquired for you but you were out. So let it all drop and do as we ask because we are very strong and we mean what we say . . ."

The article stated that when the hotel owner replied begging for more time, he received the following response:

"Dear Friend . . . We received your letter, and we are not satisfied. You are older than us, but you are not smart as us, because we have done nothing else but being brigands and crooks. We are the biggest company in Europe. We trust no one. You have got to expect nothing but our madness . . . Don't get mad if we give you a little disturbance, because we respect you as a gentleman of wealth, but you have got nothing else to expect from us but death. Just like the ripe fruit that is bound to fall, so will you.

You and your children in a few days will be killed . . . so if you want to live and your family to live, you have still got time by sending us the money in a simple letter. Nothing else to say. I remain, the secretary of the anarchists, by order of our inspector . . .

Either money or death—last notice, and if you write send a plain letter so no one will suspect, because we think we are being watched."

Was this the same crime syndicate that Frank was dealing with? Although this group was operating out of New York City, it obviously had contacts in the Boston area as well. How else would they have known? How could they have known that Frank had at one time written to Guy about coming to America? They even knew where Guy was living in Paris and how to contact him. Someone must have overheard Frank discussing Guy and had passed on the information unknowingly or—more likely—for profit. Although the ransom demand in the telegram to Frank was not written in the same threatening language as the letters described in the newspaper, the inference was if Frank did not comply, he would not see Guy alive again.

After a quick dinner, Frank gathered the money they had collected—all $600 of it—and prepared to drive back to the city with Carlo. Many of Frank's friends who had contributed their hard-earned savings came to the house after work. Some of them even knew Guy from their days in Italy growing up together. Frank explained to them what had occurred earlier that day and he was heading back now to get his cousin.

Then something unexpected happened. They each offered to help—not just by giving money—but by making sure the exchange was actually carried out and that Guy was returned unharmed. They all wanted to go to protect Frank and Carlo, and if necessary, assure that Guy was safely released.

Five cars, loaded with fifteen men ready to fight for their friend, headed for New York City.

It was approaching seven o'clock, the time they had agreed to. The four cars followed Frank and Carlo and parked close to each other. This time, they were being watched. Hidden in a dark alcove of an apartment building a block away from the storefront address on the telegram, the old man observed them enter the neighborhood, recognized Carlo's car, but then watched in disbelief as four other cars pulled in behind them. He saw Frank exit the first car and walk toward the address he had gone to earlier in the day. In his hand was an envelope. Frank assumed Pauli would approach him on the street in front of the storefront just as he had done earlier. As he made his way across the street, Frank carefully surveyed the neighborhood, expecting to see him or hear him call out again. His friends from Mamaroneck remained in their automobiles, cautiously watching Frank and alert to any sign that something was amiss or that Frank was in trouble.

But no one showed up or spoke out.

Frank walked a few blocks in one direction, then turned and walked the opposite way, hoping the old man would see him. He was afraid to walk too far and be out of view of his friends in their cars. Still, there was no sign of Pauli or anyone else he might have sent in his place. Frank waited, but after an hour had passed, he returned to the vehicles with his friends.

When they saw him coming toward them with a dejected look on his face, they got out of their cars and asked Frank what had happened.

Were they in the wrong place? Was he sure they were supposed to meet here again tonight? Was he sure about the time? Frank reassured them that this was the plan he had agreed to with the old man after he had seen Guy. He could not understand why Pauli was not here. What had gone wrong? He thought about trying to find the place where he had seen Guy earlier in the day but rejected that idea. It was already late to be wandering around New York City. Plus, he knew that was just a temporary place they had used to bring Guy to meet Frank—not where they were holding him. He would not be there any longer. Frank decided that it would be better to just go back to Mamaroneck, try again the next day, and hope that someone would be there. He had no way to contact anyone holding Guy.

Pauli watched Frank from his hiding place.

Then, without a sound, he slipped away.

CHAPTER 18

Guy watched Pauli enter the room but immediately knew something was wrong. Instead of the good news that Frank had returned with the money—and they were now going back to make the exchange—Guy could see a look of disgust and disappointment in the old man's eyes. It had not gone as expected.

"What's the matter?" Guy asked. "Didn't my cousin come?"

"Yeah, he came. But your cousin doesn't know yet what this all means, and how much trouble you're in. Why did he have to bring four other automobiles and all those other men with him?"

Guy didn't know what he was talking about. He had seen only Frank earlier in the day, no one else, and wasn't even aware that Carlo had driven him. And now "all those other men?" Who were they? Why would Frank not come alone as he had been told to do?

"If he had come alone, or even with the friend he had come with the first time, you would be home tonight with your cousin," the old man angrily said. "It's not my fault. It's your cousin's fault," he shouted repeatedly. "Your cousin's fault!"

Guy was disconsolate. Twice in one day, he had raised his expectations that this ordeal would end and that he would leave this place and these people with his cousin. Twice in one day, those hopes were dashed. He was overwhelmed with a feeling of deep despair, not knowing how this was going to end—or if it would.

His friend Ernesto was still there. They had reached Ernesto's brother in Detroit, but his brother demanded that the men holding him bring Ernesto to Detroit before he would pay them any money. They had refused, so it resulted in a stalemate. Ernesto, too, had no idea how it was going to be resolved. As he heard what was happening to Guy, they looked at each other with sorrow and sadness at these latest developments, but each bore an expression that signaled they would get through this. They had both come so far—and through so much—they were not going to give up hope. For now, however, it meant another night under the watchful eye of Sal, who had been with Ernesto while Guy had gone to see Frank. Sal's gun was still plainly visible to both men just in case they had any ideas of fleeing.

The next morning, Frank and Carlo decided they would go back alone to the address where they had first encountered Pauli. Maybe the people holding Guy had been spooked by seeing so many men show up the previous night. The rest of their friends would stay behind and await word from Frank, hoping that this time the results would be better. They were prepared to respond if it didn't.

Carlo parked in the same vicinity he had the day before. Frank exited alone and walked toward the address that had been used as a false meeting point. Before he reached the storefront, Pauli appeared in the street and called out to him.

"Why didn't you show up last night like I asked you to?" he asked.

"I did show up at the time you said, but you were not here. I waited an hour for you," Frank quickly replied. "I didn't see anyone."

"It's your fault!" Pauli demanded. "I told you to come alone. Why did you bring all those other men with you? You have no idea who you're dealing with and what serious trouble your cousin is in."

Frank was holding the envelope with the money, and Pauli asked to see it. He knew Carlo was nearby watching. Frank showed him that the envelope had money in it but did not let him touch it or count it.

"Okay. Now I'll get your cousin and bring him here. Meet me at this address in an hour." He gave Frank a slip of paper with an address. "If you have all the money, you can take your cousin."

Carlo drove Frank to the address they had been given for the exchange. It was an Italian bakery not far away. Frank went in and was told to go down to the cellar and wait there.

"Someone will come for you soon," he was told.

Guy nervously awaited for Pauli to return. He had seen him leave earlier that morning without any explanation, hopefully for another attempt to make the ransom payment. Guy had slept fitfully, not knowing whether this would be his last night in the house, or if there would be other complications. What if Frank brings all his friends again? What if he isn't able to gather all the money? How long would these people wait?

He and Ernesto discussed the seriousness of their individual situations as much as they could, but Sal was always close by, listening to everything they said. They had been in America six days now but seemed no closer to freedom than when they arrived. It had been only twelve days since they left Paris, but so much had happened to them since then. It felt like so much longer. When would it end? More importantly, how would it end?

The old man stormed into the house in a hurry and spoke to Guy.

"Your cousin is here now and waiting for you. If he has the money, you'll be set free."

Elated at the prospect of finally leaving his latest prison, Guy said good-bye again to Ernesto. The two friends embraced warmly, remembering how they had relied on each other to get through this ordeal. Sadly, neither one knew when they would see each other again. Ernesto would be in Detroit. Guy would be in Boston. Although they didn't know exactly how far they would be from each other, they knew it was quite a distance, and their visits—if any—would be few.

Guy walked close behind Pauli and followed him into a different section of the city, this time to what appeared to be a bakery. He was led down to the cellar of an old building, where he smelled fresh bagels and saw assorted cakes placed neatly on shelves. There was no activity in that part of the bakery, and no one seemed to be in the cellar. Then he was led to a corner behind several racks of baked goods.

Sitting at a table alone was Frank with a big smile on his face, as if to say, "I told you I would come back for you!" Guy beamed appreciatively and was so full of joy he was speechless. Could his long journey truly be close to an end? Could this really be happening? Was this time actually going to end well?

Frank stood and hugged his cousin, enthusiastically kissing him on both cheeks, celebrating his potential release. The moment became etched in Guy's memory. Afraid to say anything to spoil it or endanger the reality of what was happening, Guy eagerly returned his cousin's embrace. He watched as the old man carefully approached the table. He saw Frank hand an envelope to Pauli, who cautiously counted out the contents. It was all there—$600—just as they had demanded. Guy was amazed that his cousin had been able to gather that much money in such a short time, but he would save his questions for later.

As soon as the money had changed hands, Pauli's serious demeanor changed dramatically. He became their friend. He smiled at Guy and spoke to him—not as his hostage, but as if they were now *paisanos* too. Then he took a ten-dollar bill from the cash he had just received and gave it to Guy.

"Here is your first ten dollars of American money. I'm giving it to you as my present." Then he shook hands with Guy, welcomed him to the United States, and wished him luck. Guy was shocked and speechless.

"Grazie per i soldi," was all he could manage to say. "Thank you for the money."

The old man then motioned to Frank to follow him to another corner of the cellar.

"Frank, I want to talk to you," he softly whispered.

"What do you want now?" Frank answered as he followed the man across the room. His first thought was that there was a catch to the ransom demand and that it wasn't over yet.

"Do you want to join this operation? If you give us the address of someone you know who wants to come here, we'll give you $50 for each person that we bring to the United States. They can be from France, Italy, Spain, or anyplace. But they need to have relatives here in America. If they have nobody, we don't want to bother with them."

Frank was stunned by the offer. So this is how they must have tracked down Guy. It had to be an organized racket with lots of people involved. *Why have we never heard about it?* he thought.

"No, no, no. That's not my . . ." He stopped and thought about what he was about to say. He hadn't actually gotten Guy out of there safely yet, so he chose his words wisely.

"If I have somebody that wants to come, my friends in Italy or France, I'll send you the address, and you take care of it. I don't want anything."

With that, they shook hands and said good-bye.

As Frank and Guy walked out of the bakery together, Pauli said, "I'll come and see you sometime in Newton."

"Well, okay," Frank said, once again being careful and cordial. In truth, he hoped to never see him again. "You know my address."

Frank and Guy walked quickly to Carlo's car, which had been parked nearby. Carlo was thrilled to see Guy, even though they had never met before. Without delay, they drove to Mamaroneck.

When they arrived, Guy was greeted by a large group of friends, many he knew from Italy and others he didn't know but who had helped to make his release possible. They enjoyed a festive Italian dinner together, celebrating Guy's escape and first night of freedom in America.

For the first time in what would be countless other retellings of the story, Guy told this jubilant and amazed group of friends and strangers how it had all happened. How just two weeks prior, the thought of going to America was something he had not entertained in many years. A dream he once had so often had slowly faded until it became just a memory of thoughts from long ago. Yet here he was in America. As he recalled the last twelve days, the feeling of disbelief began to subside. The dream had become a reality. Although he understood he would eventually need to deal with the legality of his clandestine arrival, he was determined to do whatever had to be done to become a productive American citizen. He could not remember being happier than he was that night with these *paisanos,* the people who had probably saved his life.

However, in the midst of the celebration, one thing continued to bother him. Guy could not shake the thought of Ernesto back in the city, still in the room with Sal and his gun. How would his journey end? He would write to him at his brother's address in Detroit and wait hopefully for good news.

However Frank had managed it—and wherever the $600 had come from—Guy was greatly indebted to these people celebrating with him that night. Although he was free in America—and even had ten dollars in his pocket—it would take him years to pay it all back. He could not foresee that in a few short months, the Great Depression would descend on America.

CHAPTER 19

As we approached the bottom of the international arrivals ramp, Marie and the young woman with her squeezed their way to the front of the group of people awaiting the arrival of their loved ones. Marie did not take her gaze off my father. "Gaetano?" she called out. Dad nodded and waved. They displayed no look of suspicion or doubt—they knew who we were and were anxious to greet us. We were strangers to them, but their smiles showed us they accepted us warmly as a part of their family.

We walked up to them. Then he reached out and did something he hadn't done since he married my mother forty-seven years prior— he embraced a woman who was not a family member. It had been fifty-seven years since he had seen Marie, but he didn't hesitate to let her know that he still cared for her as a dear friend. They exchanged cheek kisses. But Dad was not yet comfortable enough, nor confident enough, to show more emotion than that. I could tell it was an awkward moment for him. He had never been an outwardly affectionate man. However, I imagined that his heart leapt for the first time since Mom died in 1978, eight years prior. I was happy for him.

Marie did not speak English, but fortunately, she spoke Italian fluently. Dad was able to converse with her in his native tongue, as most of the French language had left him many years prior. She introduced the young woman who was accompanying her as her daughter, Liliane. Dad introduced me to both of them, and I spoke enough Italian to tell both of them how glad I was to finally meet them. But I was very relieved when Liliane said I would meet her husband later and that he spoke English quite well. Knowing that I would not have to spend the entire weekend fumbling with my unpolished and broken Italian, I finally relaxed and did my best to understand what they were saying to me.

Marie was visibly thrilled to see my father. She had been looking forward to hearing his stories—and sharing hers—since they started planning this trip. But first, we would go to their house and have lunch together. Excitement shone in Dad's eyes as he anticipated finally getting answers to the questions he had pondered for decades.

It took only twenty minutes for Liliane to drive us from Orly Airport to Choisy-le-Roi, the suburb of Paris where they lived. Choisy was a charming village with lovely residential neighborhoods and tree-lined streets. Driving north from the airport, I could see the outline of the Eiffel Tower in the distance. The Seine came into view as we approached the village, and never having been to Paris, I was absorbed in the novelty of the stunning architecture and picturesque landscapes out the window. Dad probably noticed how much it had changed in sixty years, but his primary focus was on Marie as they chatted happily in the back seat. This was a reunion he had never imagined would happen.

Their attractive single-family home located on a quiet street was typical of a traditional French provincial house with the steeply pitched roof. The roof sloped downward, and there were four delightful little dormers extending beyond the roof's edges.

The interior of the house matched the rustic look of its exterior design, with hardwood flooring, ceilings accented with wooden beams, skylights, and large windows to let in abundant natural light. An arched doorway led out to a well-manicured courtyard patio with a dining area and flower garden. Upstairs were two small, comfortably decorated bedrooms that they had prepared for our stay.

Dad and I were both exhausted from having had little sleep on the all-night flight from Dallas, and the nine-hour time zone change from Southern California, where we had begun our trip. Dad lived all his life in the same town in Massachusetts but had flown to Los Angeles to visit us before we began our trip together. The jet lag was already having its effect on me, so I was very happy when Marie suggested we rest after lunch. Liliane's husband would be home in a few hours, and we would gather again for a long-anticipated dinner. I looked forward to meeting him and having someone I could speak to in English, at least momentarily ending my struggles with the language differences. It wasn't bothering Dad at all. He and Marie were doing just fine communicating in Italian. While I could understand most of what was being discussed, I couldn't add much without embarrassing myself.

Several hours later, I forced myself out of a deep sleep, my body still trying to recover. The scent of a brewed pot of strong coffee and freshly baked French pastries overcame my desire to stay in bed. I shaved, showered, and followed my nose to the kitchen, where I found Dad already sipping coffee, engrossed in a discussion with Marie. A large pot of Italian sauce slowly simmered on the stove.

Liliane's husband had just come home, and we hit it off immediately. We became absorbed in our own discussions, sharing stories of our jobs in aviation.

Glancing into the living room, I saw my father and Marie still seriously engaged in a lively discussion, presumably beginning to tell each other the events that had occurred in their lives over the last fifty-seven years. She had heard parts of his story by now from mutual friends in America and from recent letters she and Dad had exchanged. But she had never heard the details of how he had made it to America. He didn't know anything at all about what happened to her.

They would have lots of time for Dad to tell her about the events of March 5, 1929, the days that followed, and why he had left Paris so suddenly. Right now, dinner was on the table, and it was time to just enjoy each other and the blessing of being able to be together after all these years.

We spent the next few hours around the dinner table, getting acquainted with each other and with Jean-Claude and Liliane's young son, Florent, and with Marie's teenage granddaughter, Delphine. They also spoke a little English, so it was stimulating for me to have others with whom I could easily converse.

Marie beamed with joy, wearing a pretty blue and white patterned dress, and Dad looked sharp in his blue shirt and burgundy sweater. She had prepared an Italian dinner of homemade pasta for my father.

The sweet smell of the fresh sauce that had been bubbling all day lingered in the air, stimulating my already elevated appetite. It was both my father's and my favorite dish. We felt as though we were family. My father could not have been happier that this day had arrived.

After dinner, we settled into the living room, and I watched as Dad and Marie continued to tell each other about their lives. Earlier in the day, I heard him tell her about my mother, the love of his life, and how she had died abruptly of a heart embolism when she was only sixty-three years old. They had been married thirty-nine years, and it ended tragically that horrible day, eight years prior. Just before that day, they had spent several days visiting us while we were living in Connecticut to celebrate the first birthday of our daughter Nikki, their first grandchild, with about thirty of our friends and neighbors. After the party, my mother screamed of chest pains. Mom was rushed to the hospital and died before they could get her there. Although Dad didn't have the words or the will to explain to Marie the pain he had felt that day, or in the time since, I was there with him; I knew the grief and shock he experienced. Being the nonemotional man he was, he kept it in, but he could not talk for days. I, on the other hand, was emotional like my mother. I cried uncontrollably for weeks. In just hours, we had gone from one of the most joyous days of our lives to one of the saddest.

Marie shared with us that she had been married and divorced and that her ex-husband had died five years earlier. She did not provide specifics, but I could see that the void it left in her life had been—at least temporarily—filled by my father's visit.

The next day he would tell Marie the specific events of his journey to America. For now, we were both still suffering from jet lag, and decided to call it an early evening. Sharing the details of that ordeal would be better left for when his mind would be fresh and his memory more accurate. We said good night and started toward our rooms. He looked back at her for just a brief moment, and she was looking at him—an assurance for him that this was really happening. As he climbed the stairs, I could see him pondering just how he would explain it all to her.

He also wondered if he would discover why she had not replied to any of his letters.

Guy having dinner with Marie and her family in 1986.

Marie and Guy meeting for the first time in 57 years, Choisy-le-Roi, France, 1986.

CHAPTER 20

The next morning, we woke to a sunny day, with cooler temperatures hovering around forty-five degrees, but still a good day to be outside. After a light breakfast of coffee, croissants, and other assorted French pastries, we ventured out to explore the sights of the city by car.

Dad was surprised at how much Paris had grown in the past fifty-seven years, but he still recognized many of the neighborhoods and buildings that had been there much longer than that. As Liliane drove us around, Marie pointed out locations he would easily remember, places they had gone together, and sections of town each had lived and worked in.

It was a wonderful day for my father. He glowed in delight spending time with the woman he had never expected to see again. Nothing personal was discussed while we toured, but later that evening, he and Marie sat alone and talked for hours.

Guy and Marie at Versailles in 1986.

Dad did most of the talking. Marie seemed captivated, finally hearing the entire story unfold. He walked her through the events of his journey in his usual dramatic fashion. He loved telling the story. But this time was different—she had been part of it. It made telling it much more meaningful, knowing how personal it felt for her.

He explained how it had all started so unexpectedly the day he was approached by the stranger. How difficult it had been to decide whether or not to go. How frightened he had been climbing the anchor chain of the ship. How nervous he and Ernesto were remaining hidden in the cabin. He described the shock and disappointment he felt when he discovered it had all been a lie and that he was in serious trouble with some dangerous people. Through it all, she listened in amazement to each twist and turn, at times finding it difficult to believe, but all the while knowing it was the truth.

I saw her talking seriously to him and watched as he listened intently to what she said. However, it was not until the next day, as we rode the train from Paris to Rome, that I heard Marie's story from my father. It had its own plot that kept me completely fascinated just as my father had been hearing it the day before.

During that fifteen-hour train ride—when I was not sleeping or absorbed in reading a good book—we had lots of opportunities to talk. Or should I say, I had lots of time to listen. Dad seemed relieved, eager to share the details.

He told her how conflicted he had been the night he left Paris. How it had greatly upset him that he couldn't see her to explain why he was leaving or to even say good-bye. But he had expressed those feelings to her—fear, anxiety, guilt, and the obligation he felt toward his cousin—in the letter he had written on the ship as they were steaming toward New York. He explained that as soon as he had arrived in Newton by train the day after his successful rescue from the mob, he added his cousin's return address to the letter he had tucked away in his pocket and mailed it off to her in Paris. He anxiously waited for a response—but when it didn't come, he assumed it had never reached France. So he wrote to her again. Then again, several months later.

Why had he never received a reply? The answer completely stunned him.

She never received any of the letters.

To her, it was as if he had just disappeared from Paris and from her life. She heard from some of his closest friends that he had left suddenly, but none of them knew why, or how. The rumor being circulated was that he had gone to America. She didn't know if this was true—and if it was, whether it was something he had planned in advance. Certainly, you could not decide in just one day to buy a ticket and get on a ship bound for the United States. Not knowing anything about the stowaway scheme at the time, she wondered why he had not told her. Having no way to contact him, she assumed that he did not want to be contacted. If he had, surely he would have written to her.

But she never heard from him.

Initially, she was hurt and saddened by the way their time together had ended, but she moved on with her life. In just over two years from the day he left, Marie married a man she'd met a few months after my father had vanished from her life. She was only eighteen years old. Any thoughts of Gaetano had, by then, faded. But every so often, she would think of him and wonder what had happened. What had she said or done that caused him to leave without an explanation?

As she continued to describe the events of her life, what he learned lifted his spirits in some strange way. He was relieved to know her silence was not born of anger, though this knowledge also brought on more questions and feelings he could not explain.

During those early years after he had arrived in America, he sometimes wondered how she could have broken off contact with him so easily. Once he met my mother and eventually married her, he had put those thoughts behind him. His life had turned out well: he had married a woman he loved and became part of my mother's large Italian family and network of wonderful friends. He carried no regrets about the choices he had made. But those choices could have been so different if she had written back and offered him another option. While he didn't believe life could have been any better for him, would he have chosen any differently if she had responded to his letters? Would he have tried to return to France?

As the train continued through the Alps and into the more familiar scenery of the Italian countryside, he went on with her story. Marie explained to him that after he had left Paris, her father had also heard the rumors of him going to America. He convinced Marie's older sister to conspire with him to keep Marie from communicating with Guy. Her father had always been troubled by the age difference between the two—almost eleven years—and Marie's older sister was concerned that if Guy had actually gone to America, Marie might join him there. So together, they devised a plan to keep her from receiving any mail sent from Guy. When the letters arrived—and with the cooperation of their local postman—they would intercept them, and Marie's mother would hide them away, and ensure that Marie would never see them. After six months, they stopped arriving.

After Marie's father died in 1965—more than thirty-six years later—her older sister confided in her that she had been responsible for the sadness and anxiety that Marie suffered during those first few months after Guy disappeared. She admitted to Marie that she and her parents hid the truth—and the letters—from her younger sister. At the time, it seemed like the reasonable thing to do. They were merely trying to keep Marie from being hurt any further. Her sister said she was protecting Marie from making any rash or impulsive decisions that a teenager might make to follow an older man whose motives and intentions were questionable.

Then Marie told him something he had not expected to hear.

After admitting the truth, Marie's sister handed her a box with the letters that Dad had sent to her. Marie's mother had carefully kept them hidden and safe all those years.

Not only had she learned the truth—she had read each letter.

Marie and Guy had gone on to live separate, productive lives. They had raised their own families, experienced happiness, and endured struggles. Through it all, they never knew what had happened to the other. That is, until Marie read the letters almost thirty-six years after Guy had mailed them.

Now, after fifty-seven years, Dad was able to put the missing pieces together.

When Marie learned of the letters, she was distraught and disappointed with her family, but it was too late by then. She could have written back—if she could even find out where he was at that time—but she was married and assumed my father had married as well. No, she would not try finding him now.

However, she could not help but wonder what difference it would have made to him if he had received a reply from her back then. Would he have done things differently? Would he have tried to come back to Paris, and to her?

Dad did his best to answer her questions. He explained why he stayed. It was not a decision he had the luxury of making—should I stay, or should I go back? He had no money, so he had no choice. Dad wasn't happy the first few years after he arrived in America because of the money he had to repay, the lingering effects of the trauma he had experienced getting there, and the difficulties he faced during the Depression. He knew that it was better than what his family was experiencing in Italy, but he wasn't sure if life would have been this difficult in Paris. Maybe it would have been easier for him emotionally if he had heard from Marie. But it would not have made any difference in the choices he had to make. Even if he wanted to return, the situation dictated that he stay in America, at least for some time.

He had started life in the United States with no money—other than the ten American dollars the gangster had given him—but facing a $600 debt to pay to his cousin and the friends who had rescued him. Although they hadn't given him a deadline to repay the money, he imposed one on himself. He would pay them in full before he even thought of going back. The debt he was facing was more than he could expect to earn annually as a laborer during the Depression. He felt fortunate if he could earn ten dollars a week as an unskilled worker—minimum wage then was twenty-five cents an hour. Of course, at the time, the price for breakfast at a cafeteria was only twenty cents for orange juice, fried eggs, bacon, toast, and coffee. Many people were so destitute they could not even afford that. His cousin Frank and his wife had agreed to let him live with them rent free and kept him clothed and fed until he could earn enough to pay his own way.

Within a year he had earned enough money to have some semblance of a decent life in America. Whenever he could save some, he put it in the bank. The Great Depression had begun, and at just about the time he was able to live on his own—on October 29, 1929—the stock market crashed. Guy had already rented a room in a boarding house while continuing to work at low-paying jobs, putting away whatever he could. As he struggled to save money, another difficult and unexpected event jolted him.

His bank failed. He lost most of his meager savings and had to start all over.

It would not have been a simple decision for him to return to Paris, he explained. Even if he did not have the debt to repay, to leave the United States, he would have to turn himself in to the authorities and face deportation. He could also face the prospect of a jail sentence. In 1929, the United States criminalized undocumented immigrants for the first time. Before then, there were quotas in place for immigration—loosely enforced with threats of possible deportations. It was now a federal crime to enter the country illegally.

There was no way he could simply get on a ship and go back—unless he wanted to try being a stowaway again, which he felt was out of the question. By the time he had saved enough again to pay back his debt, he had already met my mother. They married in 1939, and he could apply for naturalization through a complicated waiver process. He was thoroughly vetted by the US government. His bosses and neighbors were required to vouch for his character and work ethic. It was determined that he had been in the country to earn an honest living with no criminal record or activities. He was allowed to stay.

Dad told Marie the rest of his story. In May of 1940, he was escorted to Montreal, Canada, and allowed to enter the country legally by train at St. Albans, Vermont. He proudly shared with Marie one of the highlights of his life—becoming a US citizen on August 29, 1944, at the age of forty-two. Dad had taught himself to read and write English and swore an oath of allegiance to his new country. He had worked his whole life, asking nothing of his new country except an opportunity to succeed on his own. It had graciously given him that.

The perilous journey he had begun as a stowaway in Paris in 1929 had ended with his citizenship in 1944. Although it had taken fifteen years, he told Marie, on that day in 1944, he realized it was worth all the anguish, fear, uncertainty, and risk he had endured. He was now an American, and his children would grow up with opportunities he had never had.

He knew he had made the right choice.

Left: Dena and Guy on their wedding day - February 19, 1939 (with Dena's brother Richard, best man, and her sister Ann, maid of honor). Right: Gaetano's original US Citizenship Certificate dated August 29, 1944.

Guy and Dena on their 25th wedding anniversary, 1964.

EPILOGUE

Dad did not see his family in Italy again for twenty-five years after he left the farm in 1923 in search of *la strada nuova*—the new way. He had found it. He wrote to them regularly—included money whenever he could—and was excited to receive letters back from family members who could write. They missed him terribly but were happy for him as he shared stories about how his life in America had turned from his auspicious arrival in 1929 to his marriage in 1939 to his naturalization as a US citizen in 1944. He told his family how he initially struggled with life in America during the Depression, working as a construction laborer. The work was hard, and the debt he owed his cousin and his friends continued to drain his meager paycheck. Often, he was the brunt of cruel jokes and the target of derogatory names Italians were called back then. But through all the challenges he faced, he was happy, and relayed that optimistic attitude to his family back in Italy. Guy was glad he was in America, living a life so much better than the life they had—and the one he would still have, had he stayed. He kept any complaints to himself.

He met Dena while living as a boarder at the house her parents—also from Italy—rented out to earn extra money. It was a two-story house built in 1900 as company housing for a shoe factory down the street that employed many residents in the neighborhood. Behind the house was a large, lush garden where her father grew delicious vegetables to feed his growing family—plump, juicy tomatoes, sweet yellow corn, lettuce, zucchini, peppers, and so much more. Guy rented a room on the first floor and shared it with a friend. Dena and her seven sisters and two brothers—ranging in ages from two to twenty and all born in that house—lived in two small rooms in the finished attic. Dena was the oldest, so she was forced to quit school after the seventh grade, work in the shoe factory, and help raise her sisters and brothers. Her parents and her grandmother shared the second floor. While Guy was comfortable living there, fifteen people under one roof was tight.

He was welcomed into the Italian community in Newton, where many of his friends were from his hometown in Italy. Between these *paisanos* and Dena's friends and family living in the Italian section of Framingham, a town twenty miles west of Boston, he found a family to embrace—a warm and loving substitute for the one he had left behind.

They soon started dating. Once again, Guy was the older man—he was now thirty-three years old, and Dena was only twenty—but Dena's mother and father weren't bothered by it, as Marie's parents had been. They had grown to like Guy and knew him to be a man of strong character—a good catch for their daughter. However, after a year of pleasant courtship, one event almost torpedoed their relationship.

Guy had taken her to a picnic in Newton with a large group of his Italian friends. After an hour, Dena became bored with the gathering and asked him to take her home. She did not speak Italian very well, and what little she did know was a different dialect. She could not understand the conversations and comradery that Guy was enjoying. But it was important to him. These were some of the same people who had helped rescue him in New York. He wanted to stay. After another hour, Dena went to the car and began beeping the horn. Guy was so embarrassed in front of his friends that he angrily drove her home, dropped her off, gathered his belongings, and didn't see her again for about a year.

Dena was heartbroken. She felt she had made a terrible mistake and had acted selfishly. Deciding to learn the Italian language, she took classes to improve her conversational skills. She missed Guy so much and needed to find a way to get him back in her life. Telling friends that she was now dating another man, she hoped Guy would find out. He did, and it didn't take long for him to realize the mistake he, too, had made. They rekindled the relationship and married a few years later when Dena was twenty-four years old and Guy was thirty-seven.

While their marriage thrived, their attempts at having children did not. It was not until Dena shared their problem with a doctor friend—a regular customer at the restaurant where she waitressed—that hope reappeared once again. He suggested she try some fertility treatments.

Ten years after they were married, Dena and Guy welcomed their first child into the world, a son—me. Three years later, my sister Patty was born. For my father, the life he had been hoping for in America was becoming a reality.

In 1949, a year after I was born, he flew back to Italy for the first time since he left. It was just in time to see his ailing father before he passed away the following year at age seventy-six. Dad would not return to Italy for another eleven years, and when he did—with his wife and two young children—not much had changed on the farm from when he left in 1923. There was still no running water, no toilet facilities, and only one light bulb to turn on at night. Compared with his life in America in 1960, it really was the place referred to as the *Mezzogiorno*, the "land that time forgot."

Fortunately, one of Dad's half-brothers, Arduino, worked for the state-owned railroad in Rome. He had saved enough money to purchase a small apartment building in the suburbs of the city, and we spent much of our trip there—a small village where living conditions were much improved from the primitive existence on the farm. Electricity, hot running water, indoor toilets!

We strolled through the outside markets, which were set up each day where street vendors sold everything from fruit to fish to footwear. The wonderful aroma of pizza, pastries, Italian bread, and fresh-cut flowers was a delight to my senses. I felt as if I was living like a real Italian, and I came to love and appreciate my heritage even more. I even enjoyed living on the farm—as difficult as it was—driving a horse-drawn carriage, feeding pigs and chickens, and picking luscious grapes from the vineyard that Dad's father had left him. Milk cows noisily slept in the small wooden shack—*the barraca*—in the room next to mine. In spite of the inconveniences, I fell in love with my father's Italian family, and after spending two months living with them, I cried like a baby when we had to return home. I was twelve years old, but I wanted to stay. Although most of them are gone, my memories of them are a clear and precious part of my childhood. I am still very close to my cousins living in Italy and visit them often.

In America, we lived in a two-story house (the second story being a small, finished attic) that Dad rented across the street from where my mother grew up. In 1962, Dad bought that house with a mortgage—another huge risk for him—and paid it off in twenty years. He truly achieved the American dream. Until he was sixty-five years old, he worked as a manual laborer, on various construction jobs, and rarely changed employers. He belonged to the laborer's union, so his wages continued to rise with better union contracts and his benefits improved, but the arduous work never changed. It just became harder as he grew older.

Dad's cousin Frank became a brother to him in America. Not only had he rescued my father from the clutches of the mob, possible deportation, and perhaps fates even worse, Frank housed and supported my father until he could become independent. After Frank married a woman from their hometown in Italy, he moved from Newton to Providence, Rhode Island, into the conclave of the city known as Federal Hill, where everyone and everything was Italian. At least once a month, we visited "Uncle Frank" in Providence, an hour's drive from our home in Massachusetts. He and Virginia had no children, so they lavished us with love—and toys—each time we visited. Frank died in 1968, at the age of sixty-four, while I was away at college in Colorado. I could feel my father's grief as he shared his loss with me on the phone. I grieved as well.

After our trip to Paris together in 1986, my father kept in touch with Marie by exchanging letters several times a year. In one of the early letters, Marie asked him if he would consider coming to live near her in France. Touched by the invitation, Dad responded that while he would like to be closer—and see her more often—he had too many ties holding him here. His family was in America—his daughter, his son, and especially his young grandchildren. While he would enjoy living in Paris again, he couldn't leave them behind in this late stage of his life.

He then asked her if she could come here and live in the United States. Marie responded in pretty much the same way, telling him she, too, had a life—close family and dear friends in Paris—and it would be difficult for her to leave them and start over in a new country. They both realized their time had passed and the possibilities that existed once long ago were not available to them any longer. They would, however, see each other one more time.

For a few years after their adventure together, Dad and Ernesto kept in touch. Ernesto told my father in a letter that after they parted for the last time the night Dad was rescued, it took another week for his brother to work out the details with the mobsters. Ernesto's brother finally came to New York and took him back to Detroit, where he lived and worked as a cement finisher, eventually owning his own successful business. After the grueling ordeal they shared, Ernesto, too, had achieved the American dream. He married in 1934 and raised four children. His many grandchildren still share pride in and gratitude for their grandfather's legacy.

Rose and Ernesto Zaino on their wedding day, 1934 - Ernesto is on the right

Although he didn't know all the details, my father learned Ernesto had been allowed to reenter the country legally within a year of their arrival. He became a naturalized citizen of the United States in 1948. Ernesto died in December 1986 at the age of eighty-one.

My father never saw Ernesto again after they said good-bye to each other that night in Pauli's house in 1929.

His trip to Italy after seeing Marie in 1986 would be his last. His health began to fade. He struggled with leukemia. In December 1989, he fell in his apartment and was not discovered for several hours. He was found on the floor and was taken to the ER and admitted with pneumonia. It was evident that he could no longer live alone. So, at age eighty-eight—in January of 1990—he moved into a nursing home about two miles from his house.

Still able to write, he told Marie all about it. She was so worried about Dad's health that she and her daughter flew from Paris to visit him in May of 1990. It was a joyous day for him. My sister and I accompanied Marie and Liliane for a day out to a park not far from his home.

Marie and Guy during their last visit together, May 1990

That day in May was the last time Marie and my father ever saw each other.

Later that year, Dad's health deteriorated rapidly. In September, my wife Judy, our children, and I flew from California to take him to a family reunion. He loved seeing everyone—and like a good Italian, he especially enjoyed the food! They were feeding him only blended food at the nursing home, but I told him he could eat whatever he wanted. And he did. It was his last real Italian feast, and he savored every bit of it.

In June of 1991, we were told we needed to come see him again. Everyone could tell he was nearing the end.

He hung on until August 1991, when we were called again to get out there right away. We hurriedly flew out and were so grateful to be able to see him while he was still awake and alert. He knew his children and grandchildren were there by his side.

Although he could not move his body very much, he was able to understand us and speak a few words. I will never forget the moment a priest walked into his room to administer the Last Rites, a sacrament of the Catholic church. Dad's eyes glowed with a sense of hope and excitement that I hadn't seen in years. I watched in amazement as he effortlessly sat right up in bed. I believe he saw the Lord coming and was ready and anxious to go with him. After that moment, a sense of peace appeared on his face and his condition seemed to stabilize. We rushed back to California to get more clothes and plan for a longer stay. The next day—on August 9—my sister called with the sad news.

Dad had passed away peacefully in his sleep.

He had courageously waited until he could see his grandchildren one more time. Then once we left, he went to be with God.

His incredible journey here on earth was over, but his legacy lives on. He left his children with a part of him—his bravery, integrity, fortitude, and sense of adventure. Guy's powerful spirit was passed on to each of them, and to all his descendants who wouldn't be here if he hadn't gone with the stranger that night in Paris and climbed aboard the boat.

In them is a strong connection to his humanity—his work ethic, his devotion to family, his faith—but especially, the drive to live a better life.

Granddaughter Nikki DeSantis with her Nonno, June 1991

Gaetano DeSantis (February 21, 1902 – August 9, 1991).

ACKNOWLEDGMENTS

Had it not been for my father's clear recollection of the events of March 5, 1929, and those leading up to his rescue and release twelve days later, this story could not have been written. I am forever grateful for that precious video he allowed me to record in 1984. He provided the heart for his story and the passion behind my attempt at effectively capturing its soul. Thank you, Dad.

Without Marie Folcarreli's invitation to Paris in 1986 and her enthusiastic cooperation in explaining all the details of her life after my father left, we may have never learned the truth. Although Marie died at the age of eighty-nine in 2002, I saw her two more times after that first memorable trip. The information I was able to gather from those visits was a major contribution to this story. Thank you, Marie, for being a part of my dad's life, and his story.

Thank you to Marie's daughter, Liliane, and her husband, Jean-Claude Turlier, who hosted Dad and me on our initial visit with Marie and again during the writing of the book. Their assistance was critical to my research, and they eagerly responded to my many requests for information. They provided me with numerous pictures and names of people, allowing me to fill many of the gaps in the story. *Merci pour votre amitié!*

I greatly appreciated the assistance of Ernesto Zaino's family, their enthusiastic support for the project, and their gracious permission to allow me to use the stories and pictures of Ernesto in the book. My sincere thanks go out to Dick and Nancy Zaino, Dean and Tammy Zaino, and Nick Philips. Their priceless contributions can be found in the Notes at the end of the book.

I am forever indebted to the doctors and nurses at the ICU at St. Lucie Medical Center in Florida. They rapidly and accurately responded to my ischemic stroke two years ago and skillfully managed my care for ten days. The talented therapists and staff at Encompass Rehabilitation Hospital in Stuart then patiently and proficiently brought me back to a functional level of health over the next seventeen days. Without the contributions of these dedicated people, I would not have been able to even consider writing this. You know who you are, and I thank each of you.

I want to convey my deep appreciation to the many other people who have contributed to this project. Without them, I would still be seeking guidance on the craft of writing or the motivation to finish it.

To my writing coach, the famed novelist Jerry Jenkins (the Left Behind series, and over two hundred others). His invaluable Nonfiction Blueprint online writing course allowed me to have a daily dose of tips, suggestions, and support before I started writing each day.

To DiAnn Mills, an accomplished fiction novelist as well (*Firewall, Facing the Enemy*, etc.), who gently edited my very first chapter and encouraged me to continue to learn and write.

After reading Hannah de Keijzer's book—*How to Enjoy Being Edited*—Hannah became instrumental as my coach, mentor, and developmental editor, helping me structure the manuscript correctly. She really did teach me how to enjoy being edited.

I was also very fortunate to be introduced to Laura Kaiser at Word Haven Editorial, who—as her website promises—became my expert partner in nonfiction editing. She not only identified and corrected errors, but her brilliant suggestions and creative comments on structure, transitions, pacing, and flow also added a special spice to the story.

Many thanks to Jennifer Bisbing, who provided her technical expertise in proofreading to help put the manuscript into its shiniest form.

My team at Girl Friday Productions, Georgie Hockett and Kim Kent, guided me professionally through each stage of the complicated publishing process, from an exquisite cover and interior format to photo layout and website design.

To my "Redinklings" reading group at Palm City New Hope: Pastor Gary Durham, Pastor Diane Rudd, Rose Arndt, Jeannine Voisinet, and Hugh Vickery. Our weekly meeting and read through of our most recent chapters were a highlight of my week and a continuing source of support and motivation. I wish Pastor Durham and Hugh Vickery great success with their new and exciting books!

In the initial stages of writing this story, I was not sure how well it would play, so it was especially gratifying to get reviews from my early readers. After seeing only a few chapters—still in the formative stages—these friends provided great feedback and encouragement for me to keep writing. Thank you to Bob Urciouli, Al Robinson, Kevin Salvi, and Chuck and Carol Mascari for taking the time to read through the early drafts of the manuscript and for your honest and inspiring words.

The bond with my cousins in Italy gave me confidence to share the first few chapters—roughly translated into Italian—on a trip we made to Italy to visit them and to do further research for the story. My older cousins knew my father and heard bits and pieces of the story when he told it to them many years ago. The enthusiasm for the book and their reflections on his life gave me great reassurance to know it could eventually be formally translated into a book that would honor my father in his home country and among his Italian family and friends. *Grazie mille:* Eleuterio, Tina, Guiseppe, Francesca, Andrea, Simona, and Simone. One of my sixteen-year-old cousins, Leonardo, has already given a speech about his great-great-uncle's adventure. My hope is that he and his older brother, Tommaso, will gain inspiration from my father's story, especially if they ever face their own difficult decisions.

I could not write a story about the importance of *la famiglia* in my dad's life without recognizing it in mine. I am grateful to my sister, Patricia DeSantis, not only for her recollections of our father, but especially for her remembrances of our mother and the events in Mom and Dad's lives. Patty and her husband, Rick Gieringer, read some of the early material I had written and strongly encouraged me to see it through to completion.

My daughter Nicole anxiously read every word as soon as I could get it to her. She encouraged me almost daily to do the work and tell the story, constantly asking if I had written another chapter. Thank you, Nikki, for believing in me so much and honoring your father and grandfather. Thanks also to my son, David, for allowing me to extend my father's love for flying to at least one more generation by fulfilling your dream of becoming a pilot.

Lastly—but most importantly—this book is the result of the support from my partner for fifty-four years, my wife, Judy. She loved my father and spent many days caring for him. I cherished her thoughtful reading of each chapter, the many conversations we had about them, and her countless insightful comments, edits, and suggestions. But it would not have been written at all without her continual love, her confidence in me, and her persistence in urging me to write it in the first place. It was only when Judy described her idea of the first scene of the book that I finally captured the revelation of what it could be. Without her, I would not have had the vision to write the first page.

NOTES AND STORIES
BEHIND THE STORY

CHAPTER 1

My description of events during and after the Lindbergh landing are derived from my father's recollection of the event and from firsthand observational material provided in a letter posted in *Dear Abby* by John Zuckerman from Stockton, CA, on October 21, 1990. Source: *Deseret News* (Salt Lake City, UT) website, https://www.deseret.com/1990/10/21/18887390/witness-recalls-night-lucky-lindy-landed. Additional information referenced from the Charles Lindberg website: http://www.charleslindbergh.com.

References to *"Mezzogiorno, pazienza"* are from the book: Richard Gambino, *Blood of My Blood: The Dilemma of the Italian Americans*, New York: Doubleday, 1974.

Unless otherwise noted, all photographs and illustrations are from the author's family collections or in the public domain.

CHAPTER 2

The references in this chapter and all following related to the actual events relating to his life and journey from Italy to France to America are from a transcript of a video interview of Gaetano DeSantis conducted by the author on July 21, 1984, at Mission Viejo, CA. Dialogue is primarily taken directly from the transcript of that interview, although it may be changed slightly to conform to the proper use of English. My father spoke broken English with a mixture of Italian vocabulary added.

CHAPTER 3

Much of the information about the Black Hand Society in America was derived from a book by Steven Talty: *The Black Hand*, Boston: Houghton Mifflin Harcourt, 2017. In his book, Talty tells the story of Detective Joseph Petrosino, who, in the early 1900s, led the Italian squad of New York police officers assigned to rid the city of the scourge of the Black Hand.

Additional useful information was drawn from another compelling book on the subject by Paul Moses, *The Italian Squad: The True Story of the Immigrant Cops Who Fought the Rise of the Mafia*, New York: Washington Mews Books, New York University Press, 2023.

Another well-documented and informative source on the Black Hand was by John Dickie: *Cosa Nostra: A History of the Sicilian Mafia*, New York: St. Martin's Press, 2004, 164-174.

Information pertaining to the Immigration Act of 1924 was derived from the following sources:

Department of State, Office of the Historian, Immigration Act of 1924 (The Johnson-Reed Act)

A Brief History of US Immigration Policy from the Colonial Period to the Present Day

Cato Institute: August 3, 2021, Policy Analysis No. 919 by Andrew M. Baxter and Alex Nowrasteh, https://www.cato.org/policy-analysis /brief-history-us-immigration-policy-colonial-period-present-day #dillingham-commission-world-war-i-national-origins-act-1910-1930

Library of Congress Classroom Materials at the Library of Congress Immigration and Relocation in US History Italian The Great Arrival. Immigration and Relocation in US History, https://www.loc .gov/classroom-materials/immigration/italian/

References to the conditions in steerage class on cruise ships derived from:

GG Archives: The Future of Our Past Social and Cultural History, https://www.ggarchives.com/OceanTravel/Steerage/index.html and from the book by Dorothy and Thomas Hoobler, *The Italian American Family Album-Introduction by Governor Mario M. Cuomo*, New York: Oxford University Press, 1994, 103-104.

Additional information about Ernesto Zaino was provided by

email and phone conversations with his family. Upon starting the research for this book, I was able to track down Ernesto's family. After
several failed attempts to leave messages, I received a call back from
Ernesto's son, Dick, and his wife, Nancy. After convincing him that
I was hoping he could provide additional information to me for the
book I was writing, Dick graciously spent about an hour on the phone
with me. He was very interested in the book and excited that his father's story would be told as well. We planned to visit in person soon
after. After several weeks of no replies to my calls, I left a message. As
I was leaving the message, his son Dean picked up the phone and told
me that, sadly, Dick had suddenly passed away. Several months later,
Dean contacted me again and, along with his wife, Tammy, confirmed
the identity of people in some pictures I had, and added more family
stories about their grandfather to supplement the ones my dad had
told me. I am also indebted to another of Ernesto's grandsons, Nick
Philips, for providing me with additional details about Ernesto's story.

CHAPTER 4

Pictures of the SS *Paris* in this chapter are from the following website:
   http://ssmaritime.com/SS-*Paris*.htm

CHAPTER 5

Descriptions of the SS *Paris* interior and exterior layout are drawn
from:
   Miller, William H. *Picture History of the French Line*, Toronto:
General Publishing, 1997, and Miller, William H. *The Great Liners
Story*, Great Britain: The History Press, 2012, and previously cited
SSMaritime website http://ssmaritime.com/SS-Paris.htm.
   A great source of information about the ship was derived from
the author's copy of an original SS *Paris* marketing brochure entitled
"Plan-Coupe du Nouveau Paquebot—Paris," which includes a three-
foot foldout cross-sectional layout of the decks, salons, and cabins on
the ship. I unexpectedly and fortuitously came upon this relic while

browsing through the racks of old books in one of the small sidewalk bookstores along the Left Bank of the Seine in Paris while on an airline layover about twenty years ago.

CHAPTER 7

References to *"l'ordine della famiglia"* and *"la via vecchia"* are from descriptions in the book previously cited by Richard Gambino.

Much of the history and description of Saint-Galmier, France, and Badoit Sparkling Water are from a book commissioned by the Badoit Company and presented to me during our tour of the Badoit factory in March 2024. The current automated bottling process is done in a newer part of the factory grounds, but the old factory still remains today. Some of the original buildings used to house employees are still standing, although they are now used as private residences.

Peycelon, Yves, *Badoit, Une Histoire Ptilante (A Sparkling History)*, Ravières: Les Éditions du Mécène, 2016.

CHAPTER 8

Information regarding the jazz scene in Paris during the 1920s was derived from the following:

Smithsonian Institution, "Jazz Age in Paris, 1914–1940," https://www.sites.si.edu/s/archived-exhibit?topicId=0TO36000000U0G1GAK

Another source of good information was from this blog: Nomadic Matt, "How You Can Experience 1920s Paris Today," 2008, Montmartre, https://www.nomadicmatt.com/travel-blogs/experience-paris-1920s/

The source for all historical information on the immigration records of my Italian relatives are from Ancestry.com ship manifests that show passenger names, dates of sailing, arrival ports, and hometown.

Information regarding the Immigration Act of 1924 is from the Department of State, Office of the Historian, Immigration Act of 1924 (The Johnson-Reed Act).

CHAPTER 9

Much of the historical stowaway information was derived from the following article: *The New Yorker Magazine*, "The Stowaway Craze by Laurie Gwen Shapiro," January 8, 2018, https://www.newyorker.com /culture/culture-desk/the-stowaway-craze.

Other information was gleaned from previously cited GG Archives: Stowaways on Ships–A Reporter's Exposé–1928. https:// www.ggarchives.com/OceanTravel/Stowaways/1928-11-Stowaways OnSteamships.html, which cites from the article published in *The New Age Magazine*: Minna Irving, "A Human Derelict–The Stowaway," in *The New Age Magazine*, Vol. IV, No. 3, March 1906, p. 216–221.

Facts pertaining to "the padrone system" are drawn from the pre-viously cited book by Mangione and Morreale, 105–106.

Additional helpful information was found in the article from *The Beehive*, Massachusetts Historical Society, "Immigrants Needing Protection from Themselves? The Padrone System in Boston's North End," Rakashi Chand, February 10, 2016, and from the article in the on-line *La Gazzetta Italiana*, April 2019, Ben Lariccia and Joe Tucciarne, https://www.lagazzettaitaliana.com/history-culture/9076-bound-for -america-the-padrone-system-of-contract-labor-part-1#. Other facts are from the previously cited book by Gambino, 95.

In his excellent book *Blood of My Blood* (previously cited), Richard Gambino describes the economic hardships and discrimination that immigrant Italians faced at the start of the twentieth century. The US Immigration Commission report referenced is from page 339.

Ellis Island information is plentiful in books and online. Some of the resources used for facts and statistics are from the following sources: Kravitz, Danny. *In the Shadow of Lady Liberty: Immigrant Stories from Ellis Island*. North Mankato, MN: Capstone Press, 2016, and Kravitz, Danny. *Journey to America: A Chronology of Immigration in the 1900s*, North Mankato, MN: Capstone Press, 2016.

I also derived information from the research paper, Medical Inspection of Immigrants at Ellis Island, 1891–1924: Bulletin of the New York Academy of Medicine, Vol. 56, No. 5, June 1980, Elizabeth Yew, MD Department of Medicine, Cabrini Medical Center, New York,

NY, and from the US Department of the Interior, Historic Resource Study, September 1984, "Ellis Island-Statue of Liberty National Monument," Harlan D. Unrau.

CHAPTER 10

Description of Boston's North End derived from previously cited *Beehive* article from the Massachusetts Historical Society and from a publication of the City of Boston, "North End Exploring Boston's Neighborhood," Boston Landmarks Commission, 1995, https://www .cityofboston.gov/images_documents/North_End_brochure_tcm3 -19122.pdf.

Information was also drawn from the previously cited book by Mangione and Morreale, 155–156.

Accounts of previous attempts to immigrate to America by Ernesto Zaino provided by emails and interviews with the Zaino family (see above from Chapter 3).

Description of the Ciociaria region was found in the Wandering Italy blog, "Ciociaria, A Land of Ancient Silences," James Martin, March 2014 (Updated December 2022), https://www.wanderingitaly .com/blog/article/1006/ciociaria and on the Italy Review Website, Dion Protani, 23 January 2024 https://www.italyreview.com/ciociaria.html.

That site was also used for information about the town of Sora: *Italy Review*, Dion Protani, November 2023, https://www.italyreview .com/sora.html.

CHAPTER 11

Much of the description, history, and pictures of the SS *Paris* are drawn from the previously cited website SSMaritime.com: http://ssmaritime .com/SS-Paris.htm and from the previously cited GG Archives website: https://www.ggarchives.com/OceanTravel/ImmigrantShips/Paris.html.

Additional historical information about the ship was found on the *Ocean Liners* magazine website: https://oceanlinersmagazine. com/2020/04/17/paris-is-burning/.

CHAPTER 14

The story of the uprising in Mexico on March 12 is derived from *The New York Times* archived story on March 13, 1929, "General and 1,200 Men Quit Rebels, Seize Border Town; Jalisco Chief Joins Revolt; Escobar Leaves Saltillo."

In the March 12, 1929, edition of *The New York Times*, the following story appeared about the arrival of ships in New York that day: "Eleven Ships are Due from Foreign Ports; List Includes the France, Paris, Muenchen, Antonia, Albertic, Ebro, Tivives, Avon," https://www.nytimes.com/1929/03/12/archives/eleven-ships-are-due-from-foreign-ports-list-includes-the-france.html. It is assumed that similar stories also appeared in the Italian language in the *Il Progresso Italo-American* editions on those days.

CHAPTER 15

Information about Mamaronek's moviemaking history was from an article in *The New York Times*: "When Mamaroneck Upstaged Hollywood," Bruce Berman June 19, 1977, https://www.nytimes.com/1977/06/19/archives/westchester-weekly-when-mamaroneck-upstaged-hollywood.html.

CHAPTER 17

For more information about the Black Hand operating throughout America, see Steven Talley's excellent book (already cited) *The Black Hand*. The article entitled "Pay or Be Killed" is quoted from the *Boston Globe*, published on February 24, 1908, https://www.newspapers.com/article/the-boston-globe/90161959/.

CHAPTER 20

Most of the story Marie told Dad was recorded on videotape on a subsequent visit my wife and I took to Paris to visit Marie and her family in 1995. Unfortunately, on that same trip, we drove to Rome, and our car was burglarized while we were there. The video camera—and that videotaped interview—were among the items stolen. However, my wife Judy was able to clearly recall the events Marie described that occurred after my father's disappearance. Her daughter Liliane was able to confirm more of the details of the story during a visit with them in Paris in 2024, while I was writing the book.

Liliane also provided me with pictures, names of people in the pictures, dates of important events in Marie's life, and letters my father had written to Marie after their visit in 1986. Communicating with me by email, along with hosting us at their house in Choisy-le-Roi in 2024, she and Jean-Claude were instrumental in my being able to get all the facts of Marie's life and story.

Information on the wages paid during the Depression are from the US Department of Labor, Bureau of Labor Statistics Handbook (1936), p. 917 https://babel.hathitrust.org/cgi/pt?id=uiug.30112032654953&seq=935.

The source of the statistics describing the price of breakfast during the Depression was from an article in the *Atlantic Magazine*, "Lean Times in Boston: Depression and the Drys," Charles W. Morton, February 1963 issue. https://www.theatlantic.com/magazine/archive/1963/02/lean-times-in-boston-depression-and-the-drys/657985/.

Changes to the immigration laws in 1929 were from the implementation of the Undesirable Aliens Act of 1929 (Blease's Law), making it a misdemeanor punishable by up to a year's imprisonment and fines. Returning to the United States after deportation could result in a felony punishable by up to two years imprisonment and $1,000 in fines. For more information, see Immigration History at https://immigrationhistory.org/item/undesirable-aliens-act-of-1929-bleases-law/.

SOURCES

Baker, Brynn. *Life in America: Comparing Immigrant Experiences.* North Mankato, MN: Capstone Press, 2016.

Colletta, John O. Ph.D. *They Came in Ships: A Guide to Finding Your Immigrant Ancestor's Arrival Record.* Provo: Ancestry Publishing, 2002.

Dickie, John. *Cosa Nostra: A History of the Sicilian Mafia.* New York: St. Martin's Press, 2004.

DiStasi, Lawrence, (ed). *The Big Book of Italian American Culture.* Berkeley: Sanniti Publications, 1996.

Gambino, Richard. *Blood of My Blood: The Dilemma of the Italian-Americans.* Toronto: Guernica, 2011.

Hoobler, Dorothy and Thomas. *The Italian American Family Album-Introduction by Governor Mario M. Cuomo.* New York: Oxford University Press, 1994.

Kravitz, Danny. *In the Shadow of Lady Liberty: Immigrant Stories from Ellis Island.* North Mankato, MN: Capstone Press, 2016.

Kravitz, Danny, *Journey to America: A Chronology of Immigration in the 1900s.* North Mankato, MN: Capstone Press, 2016.

Lupo, Salvatore. *History of the Mafia.* New York: Columbia University Press, 2009.

Luzzi, Joseph. *My Two Italies.* New York: Farrar, Straus and Giroux, 2014.

Mangione, Jerre and Ben Morreale. *La Storia: Five Centuries of the Italian American Experience.* New York: Harper Collins, 1992.

Miller, William H. *Picture History of the French Line.* Toronto: General Publishing, 1997.

Miller, William H. *High Style on the High Seas-Passenger Ships Interiors.* United Kingdom: Fonthill, 2020.

Miller, William H. *The Great Liners Story.* United Kingdom: The History Press, 2012.

Miller, William H. *Gateway to the World: The Port of New York in Colour Photographs*. Gloucestershire: Amberly, 2015.

Moses, Paul. *The Italian Squad, the True Story of the Immigrant Cops Who Fought the Rise of the Mafia*. New York: New York University Press, 2023.

Peycelon, Yves. *Badoit, Une Histoire Ptillante (A Sparkling History)*. Ravières: Les Éditions du Mécène, 2016.

Puzo, Mario. *The Fortunate Pilgrim*. New York: Random House Publishing Group, 1997.

Raab, Selwyn. *Five Families: The Rise, Decline, and Resurgence of America's Most Powerful Mafia Empires*. New York: Thomas Dunne Books, 2005.

Sayers, John G. *The Secrets of the Great Ocean Liners*. Oxford: Bodleian Library, 2020.

Szucs, Loretto Dennis. *They Became Americans: Finding Naturalization Records and Ethnic Origins*. Salt Lake City: Ancestry Incorporated, 1998.

Talty, Stephan. *The Black Hand: The Epic War Between a Brilliant Detective and the Deadliest Secret Society in American History*. Boston: Houghton Mifflin Harcourt, 2017.

Visco, Ferdinand J., MD. *Growing Up Italian American: The Memoirs of Ferdinand Visco & The Stories of Two Immigrant Italian Families*. New York: CreateSpace Independent Publishing Platform, 2018.

www.ingramcontent.com/pod-product-compliance
Lightning Source LLC
Chambersburg PA
CBHW021200130626
46554CB00005B/1904